# Contents

# To the student

*English Grammar in Use Supplementary Exercises* is for intermediate and advanced students who want extra practice in grammar, without help from a teacher.

There are 200 exercises in this new edition. Each exercise relates to a unit or units in *English Grammar in Use Fourth Edition*, with the unit number(s) at the top of the page. Some exercises ask you to use your own ideas. You can use this book if you don't have *English Grammar in Use*, but for an explanation of the grammar points, you need to check in *English Grammar in Use*.

The grammar points covered in this book are *not* in order of difficulty, so you can go straight to the parts where you need the most practice. Where there are several exercises on one grammar point, however, the easier ones come first.

Many of the exercises are in the form of emails, notes, conversations or short articles.  You can use these as models for writing or speaking practice.

# To the teacher

*English Grammar in Use Supplementary Exercises* offers extra practice of most of the grammar points covered in *English Grammar in Use Fourth Edition*. Much of the language is contextualised within dialogues, emails, notes, articles, etc., encouraging students to consider meaning as well as form. The book can be used as self-study material or as a basis for further practice in class or as homework.

The book is designed for students who have already worked through the exercises in *English Grammar in Use* (or elsewhere) which are relevant to their needs, but who need more, or more challenging, practice. It is particularly useful for revision work.

The exercises are organised in the same order as the units of *English Grammar in Use*, and the numbers of the relevant *English Grammar in Use* units are shown at the top of each page. Within each group of exercises there is a progression from easier to more challenging, including exercises where students are encouraged to use their own ideas. The contextualised exercises can be used as models or springboards for speaking and writing practice of a freer nature.

# Thanks

The authors would like to thank Annabel Marriott of Cambridge University Press for advice and support during the writing of this new edition, and Rhona Snelling for great editing and many helpful suggestions. Also, everyone at Kamae for their creative design work.

For trying out exercises and providing valuable feedback on the first and second editions, thanks go to: students and staff at The British Council Young Learners' Centre, Barcelona, Spain, Anglo World, Cambridge, The Studio School, Cambridge, The International Language Academy, Cambridge, Lelio Pallini, Jon Butt, Cemille Iskenderoglu, Isidro Almándarez, Catherine Carpenter, Marco Palladino, Margarida C.T. Busatto, Katie Head, Aleya Mokhtar, Graham Palmer, Rob Waring.

Illustrations by: Kathy Baxendale, Humberto Blanco, Sandy Nichols, Roger Penwill, and Gary Wing.

The authors and publishers acknowledge the following sources of copyright material and are grateful for the permissions granted. While every effort has been made, it has not always been possible to identify the sources of all the material used, or to trace all copyright holders. If any omissions are brought to our notice, we will be happy to include the appropriate acknowledgements on reprinting.

The publishers are grateful to the following for permission to reproduce photographic material:

p.2TL: Rex Features/Philippe Hays; p.2CL: Thinkstock/Hemera; p.2BL: Shutterstock/ ArtmannWitte; p.2TR: Thinkstock/istockphoto; p.2CR: Thinkstock/istockphoto; p.2BR: Alamy/ Juice Images; p.3: David Hockney "Mr & Mrs Clark & Percy" 1970-71, acrylic on canvas, 84" x 120" ©David Hockney Collection: Tate Gallery p.6B: Shutterstock/ Photodynamic; p.6T: Shutterstock/Eky Studio; p.10: Thinkstock/Digital Vision; p.14: Shutterstock/gary718; p.15: Thinkstock/Comstock; p.19: Corbis/Jim Craigmyle; p.20: Shutterstock/S.Borisov; p.21: Alamy/ Colin Underhill; p.24T: Rex Features/ Rex Interstock; p.25B: Alamy/Pixellover RM 6; p.30: Alamy/Trinity Mirror/Mirrorpix; p.34: Alamy/Andrew Woodley; p.45: Corbis/Ocean; p.51: Alamy/Tetra Images; p.52: Shutterstock/Andresr; p.57: Corbis; p.63(1): Thinkstock/istockphoto; p.63(2): The Kobal Collection/Walt Disney Pictures; p.63(3): Thinkstock/istockphoto; p.63(4): Shutterstock/huntz; p.63(5): ©Succession Picasso/Dacs, London 2011, The Bridgeman Art Library/Museo Nacional Centro de Arte Reina Sofia, Madrid, Spain;  p.63(6): Thinkstock/ istockphoto; p.63(7): Thinkstock/Stockbyte; p.63(8): Thinkstock/istockphoto; p.63(9): Shutterstock/ Dave Newman; p.63(10): Shutterstock/ itsmejust; p.65: Thinkstock/istockphoto; p.68: Colorport; p.70: Thinkstock/Creatas; p.73: Alamy/Simon Holdcroft; p.83: Shutterstock/ Ljupco Smokovski; p.87: Shutterstock/Christophe Testi; p.94: Alamy/incamerastock; p.95: Alamy/Greg Balfour Evans; p.96: Alamy/Radius Images; p.99: Alamy/Paul Broadbent; p.109: Alamy/moodboard; p.110: Thinkstock/istockphoto; p.116T: Shutterstock/aquatic creature; p.116B: Shutterstock/Monkey Business Images; p.117T: Shutterstock/Minerva Studio; p.117B: Alamy/Mark Richardson.

# English Grammar in Use

# Supplementary Exercises

# Present continuous and present simple

(**I am doing** and **I do**)

**1** Complete the webpage with the present continuous form of the verbs from the box.

| hold | offer | organise | ~~perform~~ | play | sing |

---

## What's on in Hampton *this week?*

CONTACT US

GALLERY

**The Arena**
The world famous Company of Knights (1) _is performing_ a breathtaking horseback show from Wednesday to Saturday at 7.30pm.

**City Hall**
Elisa Gonzalez (2) .................... songs from Brazil, Argentina and Mexico on Friday at 7pm.

**Hampton Sports Stadium**
Hampton Juniors football team (3) .................... against a team from Germany at 11am on Sunday.

**The Pavilion**
Local jewellers (4) .................... their Summer Sale this Sunday from 10am to 2pm.

**Shoppers' Paradise** (off Main Street)
All shoe shops (5) .................... the chance to buy one pair get one pair free every day this week!

**Hampton College of Further Education**
The education department (6) .................... an open day on Thursday – discover their range of full- and part-time courses.

---

**2** Complete the sentences with the present continuous form of the verbs.

**A** JAN:   Hi, Wendy! (1) ..._Are you waiting_.................... (you / wait) for the London train?

WENDY:   No, (2) .................... (I / meet) my mother off the train from Bristol.

**B** MANDY:   (3) .................... (this music / disturb) you?

JAMES:   No, not at all. (4) .................... (I / enjoy) it.

**C** TOM:   (5) .................... (anyone / use) this room today?

ELLIE:   (6) .................... (We / have) a meeting here after lunch, but it's free now.

**D** NINA:   Why (7) .................... (those people / shout)?

FINN:   (8) .................... (They / demonstrate) against the government.

**E** BEN:   (9) .................... (you / apply) for university?

CRAIG:   (10) .................... (I / think) about it, but I haven't decided yet.

**F** SINDY:   (11) .................... (Jane / leave) work early today?

KATE:   Yes, (12) .................... (she / fly) to Brussels at five o'clock.

**G** JOSH:   (13) .................... (you / come) to the party on Thursday?

MAX:   No, (14) .................... (I / work) late, unfortunately.

**3**  Complete the description with the present continuous form of suitable verbs. Use the negative where necessary.

**Mr and Mrs Clark and Percy by David Hockney, 1970**

This is a painting of two people and their cat. Mr Clark (1) ........*is sitting*........ on a chair.
Mrs Clark (2) ........................................ near him. They (3) ........................................ at each other, but at
the viewer. Mrs Clark (4) ........................................ a long dress. Mr Clark's got trousers and a jumper,
but he (5) ........................................ shoes. Percy is on Mr Clark's lap and he (6) ........................................
something in the garden. The sun (7) ........................................ outside, but the room is a bit dark. We
can see part of a picture which (8) ........................................ on the wall behind Mrs Clark. There's a vase
of lilies on the table, and a book (9) ........................................ beside it.

**4**  Choose a picture or photograph you like and describe what is happening in it.

........................................................................................................................

........................................................................................................................

........................................................................................................................

........................................................................................................................

........................................................................................................................

........................................................................................................................

........................................................................................................................

........................................................................................................................

**5** Complete the text with the present simple form of the verbs.

# What is an eclipse?

A solar eclipse (1) ....*happens*.... (happen) when the moon
(2) ........................................ (pass) in front of the sun. This only
(3) ........................................ (take) place when there is a new moon.
It (4) ........................................ (last) for up to 7.5 minutes.

During a solar eclipse, it is dark. The birds (5) ........................................
(not sing), and animals (6) ........................................ (keep) still and quiet.
A solar eclipse (7) ........................................ (not happen) very often, and most
people (8) ........................................ (enjoy) seeing one. However, it's important not
to look straight at the sun. If you (9) ........................................ (not remember) this,
you can damage your eyes.

A lunar eclipse (10) ........................................ (occur) when the earth's shadow
(11) ........................................ (fall) on the moon. The moon (12) ........................................
(look) dim until it (13) ........................................ (come) out from the shadow.

**6** Complete the questions with the present simple form of the verbs.

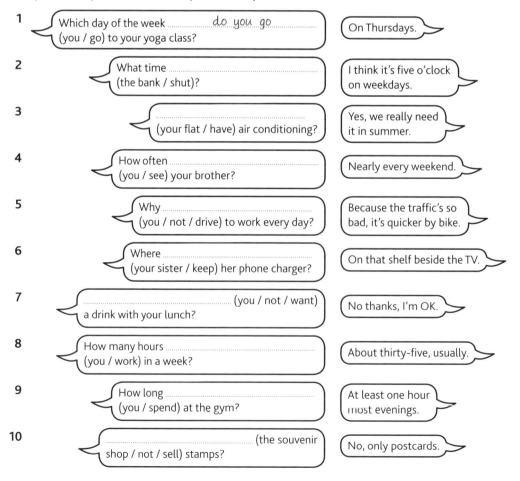

1  Which day of the week ............*do you go*............ (you / go) to your yoga class? — On Thursdays.

2  What time ........................................ (the bank / shut)? — I think it's five o'clock on weekdays.

3  ........................................ (your flat / have) air conditioning? — Yes, we really need it in summer.

4  How often ........................................ (you / see) your brother? — Nearly every weekend.

5  Why ........................................ (you / not / drive) to work every day? — Because the traffic's so bad, it's quicker by bike.

6  Where ........................................ (your sister / keep) her phone charger? — On that shelf beside the TV.

7  ........................................ (you / not / want) a drink with your lunch? — No thanks, I'm OK.

8  How many hours ........................................ (you / work) in a week? — About thirty-five, usually.

9  How long ........................................ (you / spend) at the gym? — At least one hour most evenings.

10  ........................................ (the souvenir shop / not / sell) stamps? — No, only postcards.

**7** Choose the correct alternative.

From: Pedro Martinez pm3@rygl.com
To: Kai Muller
Date: September 5, 2012
Subject: Hi from Canada

Hi Kai

(1) I'm having / ~~I have~~ a great time here in Canada. My MSc course (2) isn't starting / doesn't start until next month, so (3) I'm making / I make use of the time to get to know the place. (4) I'm staying / I stay near Vancouver with Ryan, my Canadian cousin. He and and his brother Glen (5) are owning / own a software business. In the evenings (6) we're driving / we drive into the city and go clubbing or see a movie. (7) I'm making / I make a lot of new friends. (8) I'm thinking / I think my pronunciation is much better already, and (9) I'm understanding / I understand almost everything. On weekdays (10) I'm helping / I help Glen. At the moment (11) he's working / he works on their new website and (12) he's needing / he needs help with it. (13) I'm learning / I learn some useful stuff about how people (14) are doing / do business in this country. (15) Do you come / Are you coming to see me? (16) I'm spending / I spend the winter holiday skiing with Ryan and Glen. (17) They're wanting / They want to meet you and there's plenty of space. You must bring lots of warm clothes because (18) it's getting / it gets really cold here in the winter. Let me know as soon as (19) you're deciding / you decide. And tell me what (20) you're doing / you do these days.

See you in December, I hope.

Pedro

**8** Choose words from the box and make sentences ending as shown. Use verbs in the present continuous or present simple and any other words you need.

| I My best friend My boss My boyfriend My classmates My family |
| My father My sister My wife None of my friends Our children |
| Our next-door neighbour Our teacher Several of my colleagues |

1 My boyfriend is studying for his final exams ............................................ this term.
2 My sister doesn't go to the cinema ............................................ very often.
3 My classmates aren't talking much ............................................ right now.
4 ............................................ this year.
5 ............................................ every week.
6 ............................................ at the moment.
7 ............................................ this year.
8 ............................................ at weekends.
9 ............................................ this term.
10 ............................................ right now.

**9** Put the verbs into the correct form: present continuous or present simple.

Tony Hunt, a journalist, is interviewing Leila Markham, an environmental scientist.

TONY: So tell me, Leila, why is it important to save the rainforests?

LEILA: There are so many reasons. One reason is that lots of the plants which (1) .....*grow*..... (grow) in the rainforest could be useful in medicine.

We (2) ......................................... (not / know) all the plants, but there are tens of thousands of them. Chemists and doctors (3) ......................................... (try) to discover their secrets before they are destroyed.

TONY: I see. What other reasons are there?

LEILA: Well, scientists (4) ......................................... (believe) that the rainforests

(5) ......................................... (have) an influence on the world's weather systems and this

(6) ......................................... (help) to slow down global warming. But, unfortunately, these days the forests (7) ......................................... (disappear) at a terrifying rate and we

(8) ......................................... (not / do) enough to save them.

TONY: What is the main danger of global warming, in your opinion?

LEILA: The polar regions (9) ......................................... (consist) of millions of tons of ice.

If they (10) ......................................... (melt), the level of the sea will rise and cause terrible floods. Most scientists (11) ......................................... (agree) that global temperatures (12) ......................................... (already / rise). We must do everything we can to prevent global warming, and that includes preserving the rainforests!

TONY: Thank you, Leila, and good luck in your campaign.

LEILA: Thank you.

**10** Tick (✓) the sentences which are correct. In some pairs, one sentence is correct. In other pairs, both sentences are correct.

| | |
|---|---|
| 1 What do you think of my hair? ✓ | What are you thinking of my hair? |
| 2 You look great today! | You're looking great today! |
| 3 Do you enjoy your meal? | Are you enjoying your meal? |
| 4 I think of selling my car. | I'm thinking of selling my car. |
| 5 Where do you live? | Where are you living? |
| 6 I don't believe his story. | I'm not believing his story. |
| 7 The students seem tired today. | The students are seeming tired today. |
| 8 He weighs 80 kilos. | He's weighing 80 kilos. |
| 9 How often do you play tennis? | How often are you playing tennis? |
| 10 My brother looks for a new job. | My brother is looking for a new job. |

# Past simple and past continuous

(**I did** and **I was doing**)

**11** Last week John went to Scotland on a business trip. Read his diary for last week.
Then complete the report he sent to his boss using the past simple.

| File | Edit | View | Help |
|------|------|------|------|

**6 MARCH**
**Thursday**

| | |
|---|---|
| **am** | • fly to Edinburgh<br>• have lunch with Scottish sales team |
| **pm** | • visit two factories<br>• discuss last series of adverts with marketing manager (not keen on them) |

**7 MARCH**
**Friday**

| | |
|---|---|
| **am** | • drive to Glasgow<br>• meet architects – look at new office plans |
| **pm** | • go to see new office building<br>• invite architects to dinner (not free)<br>• catch overnight train to London |

**To:** Simon Sato

**From:** John Hutchings

**Subject:** Visit to Scotland 6 & 7 March

I (1) _flew_ to Edinburgh on Thursday morning and
(2) .................... lunch with the Scottish sales team.
Then I (3) .................... our two factories there and
(4) .................... our last series of adverts with the
marketing manager. He (5) .................... keen on
them, unfortunately.

On Friday morning I (6) .................... to Glasgow
and (7) .................... the architects. We
(8) .................... at the new office plans and in the
afternoon we (9) .................... to see the new office
building. I (10) .................... the architects
to dinner, but they (11) .................... free.
I (12) .................... the overnight train back to London.

**12** Think about what you did one day last week. Complete the diary below. Then write a
report using the past simple.

| File | Edit | View | Help |
|------|------|------|------|

| am | |
|---|---|
| **lunch** | |
| **pm** | |
| **dinner** | |
| **evening** | |

**Day:**

**Name:**

On .................... morning ....................
........................................................................
........................................................................
........................................................................
........................................................................
........................................................................
........................................................................
........................................................................

**13** Use the words given to make sentences. Do not change the order of the words. Use only the past simple or past continuous.

Katie / phone / the restaurant when the pizza / arrive

*Katie phoned the restaurant when the pizza arrived.*

when Danny / arrive / we / pay / the bill

*When Danny arrived, we were paying the bill.*

while he / walk / in the mountains, Harry / see / a bear

.................................................

.................................................

the students / play / a game when the professor / arrive

.................................................

.................................................

Felix / phone / the fire brigade when the cooker / catch fire

.................................................

.................................................

when the starter / fire her pistol / the race / begin

.................................................

.................................................

I / walk / home when it / start / to snow

.................................................

.................................................

Andy / have / lunch in a cafe when Juno / phone

.................................................

.................................................

**14** Choose the correct alternative.

# Lucky accidents

Is it true that Sir Isaac Newton understood gravity because an apple (1) fell / ~~was falling~~ on his head when he (2) lay / was lying under a tree in his garden? Probably not. However, many great and small discoveries are the result of lucky accidents …

One day in 1879 chemist Constantin Fahlberg (3) didn't wash / wasn't washing his hands before dinner. While he (4) ate / was eating he (5) noticed / was noticing that the bread (6) tasted / was tasting sweet. The sweetness was saccharin.

Alexander Fleming (7) became / was becoming interested in the control of bacteria while he (8) worked / was working as a doctor during the First World War. In 1928 he (9) tidied / was tidying his laboratory when he (10) saw / was seeing that one of the dirty dishes (11) didn't have / wasn't having any bacteria on it, but that something else (12) grew / was growing there. It was penicillin.

In 1930 dietician Ruth Wakefield (13) prepared / was preparing some cookies for guests when she (14) realised / was realising that she had no chocolate powder. She (15) decided / was deciding to use small pieces of ordinary chocolate instead. The chocolate pieces (16) didn't melt / wasn't melting, and the first chocolate chip cookies were a great success.

Dr Percy Spencer was a physicist in the 1940s who probably enjoyed chocolate chip cookies. He (17) walked / was walking past some equipment in the laboratory when he (18) felt / was feeling something strange in his pocket. It was his chocolate bar and it (19) melted / was melting. This accident (20) led / was leading to the invention of a new piece of cooking equipment – the microwave oven.

**15** Put the verbs into the correct form: past simple or past continuous.

Hi Becky,

Guess what, my sister Naomi is married! She (1) ....got.... (get) home from her round the world trip last week with a husband!! She (2) ........................ (meet) him when she (3) ........................ (travel) round New Zealand. One afternoon, while her friends (4) ........................ (shop), she (5) ........................ (go) to look round an art gallery. She (6) ........................ (look) at a small sculpture when a young man (7) ........................ (come) into the room and he (8) ........................ (start) to put it into his rucksack. She (9) ........................ (call) the security guard because she (10) ........................ (think) the man (11) ........................ (try) to steal it. She (12) ........................ (be) really embarrassed to discover that he (13) ........................ (not steal) it – it (14) ........................ (belong) to him! Anyway, he (15) ........................ (not mind) and he (16) ........................ (ask) her to go for a coffee. They (17) ........................ (get married) a month later in Bali. We (18) ........................ (not know) anything about it! Can you believe it? He's really nice and they are very happy together!

Love, Ada

**16** Here is part of the website of a rock star called Colin Boyle. Put the verbs into the correct form: past simple or past continuous.

---

⋆ **COLIN BOYLE** HOME | NEWS | ABOUT | TOURS | EXTRAS

Colin Boyle was born in 1988 near Dublin, Ireland. In 2003 he became seriously ill. While he (1) *was recovering* (recover), his uncle (2) .................... (give) him an old drumkit. He enjoyed playing and practised in a friend's garage every evening. One day in 2005, John Leaf, the manager of several successful musicians, (3) .................... (pass) the garage when he (4) .................... (hear) Colin practising. He (5) .................... (bang) on the garage door and (6) .................... (invite) Colin to appear in one of the concerts he (7) .................... (organise) that year. Colin, however, (8) .................... (not accept) Leaf's invitation, because at that time he (9) .................... (prepare) for some important school exams.

Colin (10) .................... (pass) his exams and (11) .................... (go) to university to study engineering. At university he (12) .................... (meet) Kim O'Malley, who (13) .................... (study) chemistry. Kim played the saxophone. Being students, they (14) .................... (not have) much money and they usually (15) .................... (work) as waiters at weekends.

One evening in April 2008, while Colin and Kim (16) .................... (serve) customers, the manager (17) .................... (announce) that there would be no live music in the restaurant that night as the regular band could not come. Colin and Kim (18) .................... (persuade) the manager to let them play. All the customers and staff (19) .................... (be) amazed to hear how good their music (20) .................... (be). In the next six months Colin and Kim (21) .................... (earn) so much money they (22) .................... (decide) to leave university and go on tour. Their success has continued ever since.

---

**17** Complete the first sentence with the verb in the past continuous. Write a second sentence with the verb in the past simple to say what happened next. Use your own ideas.

**1** When my phone rang, I *was watching TV.*
   *I answered it but it was a wrong number.*

**2** I .................... when it started to rain.

**3** Everyone .................... when the lights went out.

**4** When we came out of the cinema, the sun ....................

# Present and past

(**I do / I am doing** and **I did / I was doing**)

**18**  Choose the correct alternative.

ADAM:    Hello, Mike. What (1) <u>are you doing / do you do</u> in my part of London?

MIKE:    Well, actually, (2) <u>I'm looking / I look</u> at these new flats (3) <u>they're building / they build</u> down the road here.

ADAM:    Well, (4) <u>they're looking / they look</u> quite cool, but (5) <u>I'm thinking / I think</u> they're quite expensive. So (6) <u>are you wanting / do you want</u> to move to this area?

MIKE:    Yes. In fact, well, the news is that Mandy and I (7) <u>are getting / get</u> married.

ADAM:    Oh, wow! Congratulations. When (8) <u>were you deciding / did you decide</u>?

MIKE:    Only last week. It was while (9) <u>we were staying / we stayed</u> with her family in Scotland. Now (10) <u>we try / we're trying</u> to find a suitable flat.

ADAM:    I hope you manage to buy one of these.

MIKE:    Oh, (11) <u>we aren't looking / we don't look</u> for one to buy. (12) <u>We aren't having / We don't have</u> enough money yet. (13) <u>We're wanting / We want</u> to rent one.

ADAM:    Yes, of course. That's what Anna and I (14) <u>did / were doing</u> at first. After that, my brother (15) <u>was lending / lent</u> us some money. That's how (16) <u>we were managing / we managed</u> to buy ours.

MIKE:    You're right. We must talk to our families before (17) <u>we choose / we're choosing</u> a flat.

ADAM:    Yeah, my family (18) <u>gave / were giving</u> us a lot of help and advice. Now, what about a sandwich at my place? It's just round the corner.

MIKE:    Oh yes, thanks. (19) <u>I looked / I was looking</u> for somewhere to eat when (20) <u>I was bumping / I bumped</u> into you.

**19**  Put the verbs into the correct form: present simple, present continuous, past simple or past continuous.

1  I remember the day you got engaged. I ....*was having*.... a shower when you phoned. (have)

2  He tried to explain his problems to his parents, but they just ........................................ what he was talking about. (not / understand)

3  What have you put in my burger? It ........................................ absolutely disgusting. (taste)

4  Mick always claimed that he was innocent, but for many years no-one ........................................ him. (believe)

5  It's a great jacket, I know, but unfortunately it ........................................ to me. I'm just borrowing it for the party this evening. (not / belong)

6  Why ........................................ that thin dress? You'll freeze to death in this cold wind! (you / wear)

7  Zoe's fed up because she hurt her ankle when she ........................................ this morning. (jog)

8  While I was admiring the view, someone ........................................ my phone from my bag. (steal)

9  Look! ........................................ that man standing at the checkout? I'm sure I know him. (you / see)

10  Tea or coffee? I'm making both, so just say which you........................................ . (prefer)

**20** There are mistakes in eight of these sentences. Correct the sentences where necessary. Write 'OK' if the sentence is already correct.

1 _The coffee is smelling wonderful._     _The coffee smells wonderful._
2 Last year we visited Australia.     _OK_
3 The ship sank because the engineer wasn't calling for help until it was too late.
4 The reason I get fat is that I'm always tasting things while I'm cooking.
5 How is Jennifer? Does her health improve?
6 You're quite right, I'm completely agreeing with you.
7 What did you after you left school?
8 Now I understand what you're trying to say!
9 I can't imagine why you were believing all those stories.
10 Martin looked forward to a quiet evening when his brother came home from the football match with ten friends.
11 Philippa heard the election result as she was driving to work, so she phoned me when she got there.
12 I'm sorry, I've spilt your drink. Where are you keeping the paper towels?

**21** Complete the email with suitable verbs in the correct form: present simple, present continuous, past simple or past continuous.

From: Alice
To: Anita
Subject: Hi

Hi Anita,

Thanks for the text you (1) __sent__ yesterday. I (2) ............... to feel better now although my back still (3) ............... if I (4) ............... too far.

Last night I (5) ............... some friends who (6) ............... dinner near here. I (7) ............... to the cafe quite easily, but while I (8) ............... home, my back (9) ............... to ache really badly. So today I (10) ............... more careful.

It's great that you (11) ............... to find that website about Indian music that you (12) ............... for. I've got some DVDs if you (13) ............... to borrow them.

I must lie down now because my back (14) ............... to hurt again. Come and see me soon. I'm OK, but you know me, I (15) ............... bored very quickly!

Love, Alice

**22** Complete the questions with suitable verbs in the correct form: present simple, present continuous, past simple or past continuous.

1 Why _are you wearing_ your coat and hat? — I'm really cold.

2 How often .................... your teeth? — Twice a day.

3 When .................... your driving test? — Last Friday. Would you like a lift somewhere?

4 .................... this programme? — No, it's not very interesting.

5 What time .................... to bed last night? — About one o'clock I think.

6 .................... this jumper is too small for me? — Not at all. It's fine.

7 What .................... at one o'clock this morning? — I was at home watching TV.

8 What time .................... ....................? — Nine o'clock usually

POST OFFICE
CLOSED

# Present perfect simple and continuous

(I have done and I have been doing)

**23** Complete the email with the present perfect simple form of the verbs.

> From: Theresa
> To: Flora
> Subject: Hi
>
> ───────────────────────────────
>
> Hi Flora
> As you can see, I (1) __'ve arrived__ (arrive) safely. Paul and I (2) ................................
> (already / do) lots of things even though (3) ................................ (I / only / be) in
> New York twenty-four hours. (4) ................................ (I / not sleep) for two days!
> (5) ................................ (I / take) about a hundred photos already.
> Paul (6) ................................ (show) me lots of famous landmarks and
> (7) ................................ (I / eat) a real American breakfast.
> (8) ................................ (I / ride) in a yellow cab and (9) ................................ (I / travel) on
> the subway too. (10) ................................ (I / not spend) any money yet because Paul
> (11) ................................ (pay) for everything so far. I'll email you some more photos
> when (12) ................................ (I / have) some sleep.
> Love Theresa
>
> 🖉 **1 attachment**

**24** Tick (✓) the sentence which means the same as the first sentence.

**1** Have you ever visited Ibiza?
   *a* Did you visit Ibiza?
   *b* Have you been to Ibiza? ✓
   *c* Have you visited Ibiza recently?

**2** This is the first time I've been skiing.
   *a* I've been skiing once before.
   *b* I haven't been skiing for a long time.
   *c* I've never been skiing before.

**3** I've had two holidays this year.
   *a* I've just come back from holiday.
   *b* I've been on holiday twice this year.
   *c* I've been away for two weeks.

**4** We've just got home from the beach.
   *a* We were at the beach very recently.
   *b* We haven't been to the beach for a long time.
   *c* We went to the beach yesterday.

**5** My manager hasn't been at work for a week.
   *a* My manager has left the company.
   *b* My manager has been away for a week.
   *c* My manager didn't come to work last week.

**6** I haven't checked my emails since this morning.
   *a* I have just checked my emails.
   *b* I haven't checked my emails today.
   *c* I checked my emails this morning.

**25**  Complete the conversation with the verbs from the box in the correct form: present perfect simple or present perfect continuous. In some cases both forms are possible. You need to use some of the verbs more than once. Read the whole conversation before you begin.

> be    come    do    drive    find    have    look

Jane is being interviewed by Nicola for a job working with young children.

NICOLA: Come in, Jane. Please sit down. Would you like a coffee?

JANE: Thank you, actually I (1) _'ve just had_ (just) one.

NICOLA: Oh good. Now, do you know this area at all?

JANE: Quite well. I've got friends who live in this town, so I (2) _____ here for holidays since I was a child. I'm staying with them at the moment, actually.

NICOLA: Oh, that's nice. And do you have a driving licence?

JANE: Yes. I (3) _____ for four years now.

NICOLA: And would you say you're a careful driver?

JANE: Yes, I think so. At least I (4) _____ (never) an accident.

NICOLA: Good. Now, could you tell me why you think you would be right for this job?

JANE: Well, I (5) _____ (always) interested in working with small children. And I (6) _____ two holiday jobs looking after children.

NICOLA: How do you think you would cope in an emergency?

JANE: I'm quite a calm person, I think. I (7) _____ a first aid course too. I got a certificate.

NICOLA: That's good. Now, this job isn't permanent, as you know. We need someone for about a year. How would that fit with your long-term plans?

JANE: I'd like to work abroad eventually. But I want some full-time experience first. I (8) _____ a Nursery Teacher's course this year. We finish next week, in fact.

NICOLA: When would you be able to start?

JANE: As soon as I finish my course.

NICOLA: Excellent. And would you live with your friends?

JANE: Well, probably not. I want to rent a small flat. I (9) _____ in the paper every day, but I (10) _____ (not) anything yet.

NICOLA: Well, if you get the job, we'll try to help you. Now, would you like to come and meet some of the children?

JANE: Oh, yes.

NICOLA: Right, if you'll just follow me then.

**26** Tick (✓) the sentences which are correct. In some pairs, one sentence is correct. In other pairs, both sentences are correct.

1 She's had a headache all day. ✓        She's been having a headache all day.
2 I've wanted a cat for a long time.        I've been wanting a cat for a long time.
3 They've eaten lunch.        They've been eating lunch.
4 I've known her for two years.        I've been knowing her for two years.
5 He's been very helpful.        He's been being very helpful.
6 He's tasted the soup.        He's been tasting the soup.
7 They've seen this movie before.        They've been seeing this movie before.
8 I've seen a throat specialist.        I've been seeing a throat specialist.
9 We've realised where we are now.        We've been realising where we are now.
10 It's belonged to us for many years.        It's been belonging to us for many years.
11 He's explained the plan to us.        He's been explaining the plan to us.
12 You've broken my phone!        You've been breaking my phone!

**27** Put the verbs into the correct form: present perfect simple or present perfect continuous.

1 John's terribly upset. _He's broken off_ (he / break off) his engagement to Megan. Apparently _she's been seeing_ (she / see) someone else while _he's been_ (he / be) in Africa.

2 Could you translate this Arabic song for me? I understood Arabic when I was a child, but ........................................................... (I / forget) it all.

3 What's that mark on the side of the car? ........................................................... (you / have) an accident?

4 The lock on this case is broken. ........................................................... (you / play about) with it?

5 Your Portuguese is very good. ........................................................... (you / study) it long?

6 Of course you don't know what I think! ........................................................... (you / never / ask) my opinion.

7 I'm not surprised ........................................................... (he / fail) the exam. ........................................................... (he / not / work) hard recently.

8 Mina's hands are very dirty. ........................................................... (she / repair) her bike.

9 I'm going to make some lunch for the kids. ........................................................... (they / swim) all morning. I'm sure they're hungry.

10 ........................................................... (I / do) grammar exercises all morning. I deserve a break.

11 Where's my phone? This is the third time ........................................................... (I / lose) it today!

12 Oh, do be quiet. ........................................................... (you / grumble) all weekend!

13 Since Maria won that talent show ........................................................... (she / spend) money like water. ........................................................... (she / buy) a new car and ........................................................... (she / move) to a big new house. ........................................................... (she / give) wonderful parties every weekend too.

In fact, I'm going to one tomorrow.

**28** Complete the sentences with the verbs in the correct form: present perfect simple or present perfect continuous.

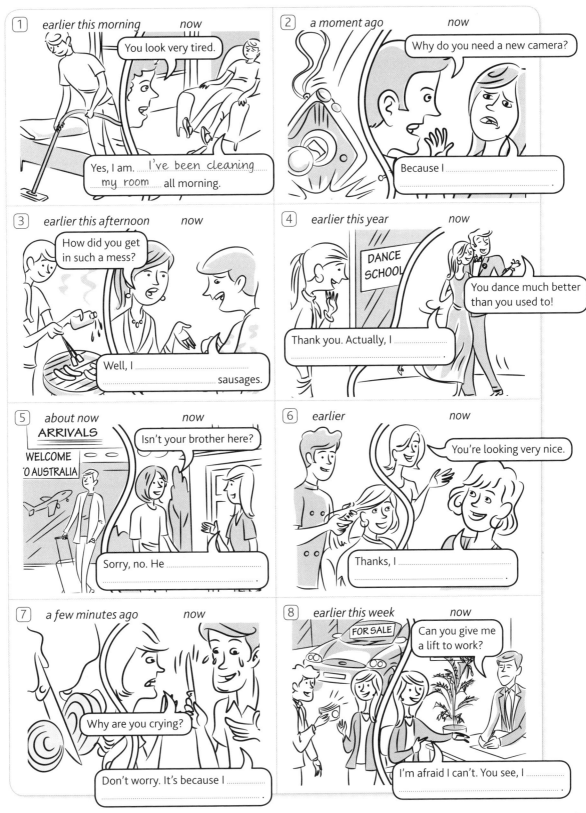

1. *earlier this morning* — *now*
   You look very tired.
   Yes, I am. I've been cleaning my room all morning.

2. *a moment ago* — *now*
   Why do you need a new camera?
   Because I .....................................

3. *earlier this afternoon* — *now*
   How did you get in such a mess?
   Well, I ................................... sausages.

4. *earlier this year* — *now*
   DANCE SCHOOL
   You dance much better than you used to!
   Thank you. Actually, I ...................................

5. *about now* — *now*
   ARRIVALS
   WELCOME TO AUSTRALIA
   Isn't your brother here?
   Sorry, no. He ...................................

6. *earlier* — *now*
   You're looking very nice.
   Thanks, I ...................................

7. *a few minutes ago* — *now*
   Why are you crying?
   Don't worry. It's because I ...................................

8. *earlier this week* — *now*
   FOR SALE
   Can you give me a lift to work?
   I'm afraid I can't. You see, I ...................................

# Present perfect simple and continuous; past simple

(**I have done** and **I have been doing**; **I did**)

**29** Complete the second sentence so that it has a similar meaning to the first sentence.

1 We haven't been to a beach party for over a year.
   The last time we ....*went to a beach party*.... was over a year ago.

2 Your wedding was the last time I wore a long dress.
   I ........................................................ since your wedding.

3 It's nearly twenty years since my father saw his brother.
   My father ........................................................ for nearly twenty years.

4 James went to Bratislava last Friday and is still there.
   James has ........................................................ to Bratislava.

5 When did you learn to drive?
   How long is it ........................................................ to drive?

6 The last time I went scuba diving was when we were in Egypt.
   I haven't ........................................................ we were in Egypt.

7 You haven't topped up your phone for weeks.
   It's weeks ........................................................ your phone.

8 We started looking for a flat two months ago and we're still looking.
   We've ........................................................ a flat for two months.

9 This is the first time I've been to a nightclub.
   I ........................................................ to a nightclub before.

10 Kim lost her job a year ago and is still trying to find one.
   Kim ........................................................ a job for a whole year.

**30** Use your own ideas to complete the sentences. Use the present perfect simple, the present perfect continuous or the past simple.

1 Since we bought this car, .*we've done lots of trips round the country.*.........
   or .*we've been doing lots of trips round the country.*.........

2 .*My colleague was ill, so I had to work overtime*........................ last week.

3 ........................................................ for several years.

4 ........................................................ since yesterday.

5 When I was a child, ........................................................ .

6 ........................................................ ten minutes ago.

7 It's three weeks since ........................................................ .

8 For the past three weeks ........................................................ .

9 ........................................................ in 2010.

10 ........................................................ since I came into this room.

11 Last December ........................................................ .

12 ........................................................ since I got up this morning.

# Present perfect and present

## (I have done / I have been doing and I do / I am doing)

**31** Choose the correct alternative.

Megan meets her friend Jess in a cafe.

MEGAN: Hi, Jess, how are you? (1) <u>I haven't seen</u> / ~~I haven't been seeing~~ you since the summer.

JESS: No, (2) <u>I've been revising</u> / I've revised for my exams. They're next week. What about you?

MEGAN: Well, a few days ago I met a website designer, Steve, (3) <u>who's looking</u> / who's been looking for some help for weeks. (4) <u>He offers</u> / He's offered me some work from next week.

JESS: That's great.

MEGAN: Yeah, and every day since then (5) <u>I look</u> / I've been looking at his sites. (6) <u>He's designed</u> / He's been designing three or four really cool ones already. But (7) <u>he doesn't have</u> / he isn't having enough time to do all the new ones. That's why (8) <u>he's needing</u> / he needs me.

JESS: That's really good. Hey, who's that guy over there? (9) <u>He's looked</u> / He's been looking at us since we met.

MEGAN: Oh, wow, that's Steve, the guy (10) <u>I've been telling</u> / I tell you about.

JESS: (11) <u>He's looking</u> / He looks like a student or something.

MEGAN: Shh. (12) <u>He's coming</u> / He comes over.

STEVE: Hi, Megan.

MEGAN: Steve, this is my friend Jess.

STEVE: Hello. (13) <u>Do you using</u> / Are you using the Wi-Fi in here at the moment?

JESS: Yes. (14) <u>I come</u> / I'm coming here most days for lunch and since the cafe's got Wi-Fi (15) <u>I've checked</u> / I've been checking my email at the same time.

STEVE: And (16) <u>do you enjoy</u> / are you enjoying the food here?

JESS: Er, yes. It's always very good. But why?

STEVE: Oh, just interested. (17) <u>I own</u> / I'm owning this cafe.

MEGAN: I didn't know that!

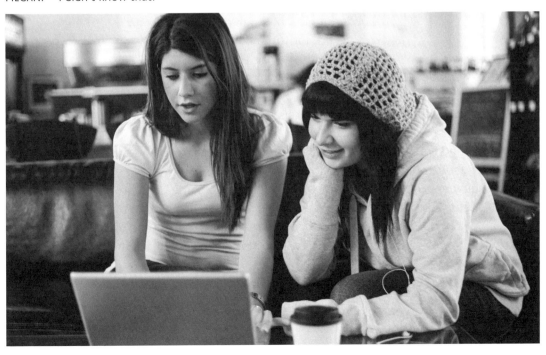

**32** Complete the sentences with the verbs from the box in the correct form: present perfect simple, present perfect continuous, present simple or present continuous.

| not / be | ~~deal~~ | ~~not / finish~~ | have | not / know | live | see | not / see |
|---|---|---|---|---|---|---|---|
| not / speak | stare | stay | suffer | wait | not / want | watch | |

1  I _haven't finished_ checking the emails because I _'ve been dealing_ with customers all morning.

2  Thank you, but I really ................................................ any more juice. I ................................................ two large glasses already.

3  Paul ................................................ from earache since the weekend.
   He ................................................ the doctor twice, but it's still not better.

4  We ................................................ why Sara is upset, but she ................................................ to us for ages.

5  Why ................................................ you ................................................ at me like that?
   I suppose you ................................................ a woman on a motorbike before!

6  I ................................................ with my cousin in London for a few days.
   I ................................................ here before, but he ................................................ here for several years, so he can show me around.

7  I'm sorry I'm late. ................................................ you ................................................ a long time?

8  We ................................................ this stupid film since lunchtime. Let's switch over to the other channel.

**33** Complete the email with suitable verbs in the correct form: present perfect simple, present perfect continuous, present simple or present continuous.

Dear Nick,
We (1) _'re having_ a wonderful time here in Prague. We (2) ................................................ here for three days now and we (3) ................................................ to stay for the rest of the week because we (4) ................................................ ourselves so much. We (5) ................................................ the Charles Bridge and the Castle, and this morning we (6) ................................................ around other historic places, including Kafka's house. I (7) ................................................ this photo just before lunch. We (8) ................................................ any souvenirs yet, but we (9) ................................................ some good art galleries and shops. Fortunately, the weather (10) ................................................ too cold so far. People (11) ................................................ it can be really bad at this time of year and of course it often (12) ................................................ heavily here! As this is the first time we (13) ................................................ to Prague, we (14) ................................................ that we're just lucky.
See you soon,
Roberto and Jan

**34** **Put the verbs into the correct form: present perfect simple, present perfect continuous, present simple or present continuous.**

Sam is the captain of his local football team. He's talking to his brother, Dave.

SAM:  Dave, I'm worried about the team.

DAVE:  But why? (1) _You've won_ (You / win) every game this season.

SAM:  Yeah, (2) ............................................................. (we / be) very lucky.
That's (3) ............................................................. (what / cause) me problems now.

DAVE:  How come?

SAM:  Well, (4) ............................................................. (we / practise) twice a week since
the beginning of this season and (5) .............................................................
(that / really / make) a difference. Now, some of the guys say that's not necessary because
(6) ............................................................. (we / always / win). The thing is, I'm afraid that
if (7) ............................................................. (we / not / practise) so often, we may start
losing matches. Like, (8) ............................................................. (we / play) Donnington on
Saturday and (9) ............................................................. (everyone / agree)
they're a really strong team. The trouble is, (10) .............................................................
(we / not / practise) since Monday.

DAVE:  I can see (11) ............................................................. (you / have) a problem.
What can you do?

SAM:  I think the problem is really Callum.

DAVE:  The big guy (12) ............................................................. (who / play) for you since last
season?

SAM:  Yeah, and (13) ............................................................. (he / usually / score) most of the
goals. The trouble is, since the summer (14) .............................................................
(he / arrive) for training really late. And now some of the others
(15) ............................................................. (begin) to do the same. When I try to talk to
him, (16) ............................................................. (he / refuse) to listen to what
(17) ............................................................. (I / say).

DAVE:  Well, you're the captain, tell him he can't play if
(18) ............................................................. (he / not / listen) to you.

SAM:  OK, but (19) .............................................................
(I / not / like) it. What if he gets angry and leaves the team?

DAVE:  I'm sure he won't.

SAM:  Yeah, well. (20) .............................................................
(I / hope) not.

# Present perfect, present and past

(I have done / I have been doing, I do / I am doing and I did)

**35** There are seven mistakes in this email. Correct the mistakes.

From: mariannanov@wtmail.com
To: maaziz@market.solutions.co.uk
Subject: Temporary manager

Dear Mr Aziz,

*I have seen*

I would like to apply for the job of temporary manager which I see advertised on your website.

I am twenty years old. I was born in Poland, but my family moved to England when I was twelve and I am living here ever since. I left school since three years and since then I am having several jobs in tourism and marketing. For the past six months I am working for Go-Places Agency. The manager has been saying that he is willing to give me a reference.

I speak Polish and English fluently. I have also learnt Spanish since I left school, so I speak some Spanish too.

I hope you will consider my application.

Yours sincerely,
Marianna Nowak

**36** Write an email applying for this job. You may write for yourself or you may invent an applicant.

## Student **jobsearch**  Temporary jobs

**Assistant shop manager – Allingham**

Busy souvenir shop seeks bright, helpful person for two months in summer.
Must speak fluent English in addition to at least one other language. Experience and qualifications not essential, but desirable. Good pay and conditions.

Email giving details + one referee to Nicole.Sparks@studentjobsearch.co.uk

To: Nicole.Sparks@studentjobsearch.co.uk

Subject: Assistant shop manager

English Grammar in Use Supplementary Exercises

# Present perfect and past simple
(**I have done** / **I have been doing** and **I did**)

**37** Match the beginning of each sentence with the most suitable ending to make a story.

| | | |
|---|---|---|
| 1 The Ocean Hotel opened | *a* half an hour ago. | 1 ___c___ |
| 2 There's been a nightclub there | *b* last night. | 2 _____ |
| 3 I went clubbing there | *c* ~~in 2008.~~ | 3 _____ |
| 4 I lost my coat | *d* since January. | 4 _____ |
| 5 I phoned the club | *e* all day. | 5 _____ |
| 6 The manager asked me to wait | *f* when I went there. | 6 _____ |
| 7 That's why I've felt cold | *g* for a few days in case it's found. | 7 _____ |

**38** Choose the correct alternative.

1 My sister <u>has been</u> / <s>was</s> interested in medicine ever since <u>she <s>has been</s></u> / <u>she was</u> a child.

2 How long <u>have you studied / did you study</u> before <u>you have qualified / you qualified</u>?

3 Where <u>have you first met / did you first meet</u> your boyfriend?

4 Is this the first time <u>you've cooked / you cooked</u> pasta?

5 <u>We've wanted / We wanted</u> to go to out last night, but <u>we haven't had / we didn't have</u> any money.

6 What can we do? I'm sure something <u>has happened / happened</u> to Alex. <u>We've been texting / We texted</u> him for over an hour and <u>he still hasn't replied / he still hasn't been replying</u>.

7 <u>We have posted / We posted</u> the new DVD to you three weeks ago. If <u>you haven't received / you didn't receive</u> it yet, please email us immediately.

8 I'm exhausted because <u>I've worked / I've been working</u> in a restaurant for the past three weeks. <u>I've never realised / I never realised</u> before how hard the work is!

**39** Complete the sentences with the verbs from the box in the correct form: present perfect or past simple.

| | | | | | |
|---|---|---|---|---|---|
| ~~be~~ | be | break | earn | forget | give |
| go | have | offer | phone | tell | train |

1 Bill ___has been___ off work all this week.

2 Gina _____ to the cinema every weekend when she was a student.

3 Pippa _____ very quiet recently. Is she OK?

4 Eric _____ every day for six months before he ran the marathon.

5 How long _____ Neil _____ his present job?

6 _____ Tina _____ her parents since she left home?

7 Ow, that hurt! I think I _____ my toe.

8 Jock _____ me about his problems last night.

9 I _____ Sue's mobile number. Do you have it?

10 Jane _____ more money in her last job, but she enjoys this one more.

11 _____ Mark _____ you his address before he left?

12 My brother _____ to lend me his car tomorrow, so I needn't get the bus.

**40** Put the verbs into the correct form: present perfect simple or past simple. Read the whole text before you begin.

# Then *and* Now

Twenty years ago only a few people (1) _realised_ (realise) how greatly technology was about to transform our daily lives. This short period of time (2) .......................... (see) enormous changes in how we live, study and work.

Trips to the supermarket which once (3) .......................... (take) half the weekend have been replaced with online ordering. Music lovers who a decade ago (4) .......................... (spend) hours wandering around shops, simply download the tracks they want to hear. Information which (5) .......................... (require) hours of research in a library (6) .......................... (become) available to anybody in a few clicks on the keyboard. The spread of laptops and WiFi (7) .......................... (enable) students and business people to work almost anywhere at anytime and mobile phones (8) .......................... (transform) the way people organise their lives.

Some of us may wonder, however, how much our lives (9) .......................... (improve) in recent years. Online banking, for example, (10) .......................... (replace) the friendly bank clerk who (11) .......................... (know) your name with an impersonal website. Teachers complain that students (12) .......................... (learn) to copy and paste instead of thinking for themselves. There are fears that governments (13) .......................... (not/do) enough to safeguard personal data held on computers. Certainly, many people may now be wondering whether modern technology (14) .......................... (bring) us as many problems as it (15) .......................... (solve).

**41** Alex wants to go to an art college and is being interviewed by Tom Smith, one of the lecturers. Complete the questions which Tom asks him. Read the whole conversation before you begin.

TOM: Right, Alex, let's find out something about you. When (1) _did you leave_ school?

ALEX: Five years ago, actually.

TOM: And where (2) .......................................... since then?

ALEX: Well, I've had several jobs.

TOM: What (3) .......................................... first?

ALEX: I worked in a cafe for about a year. I needed to save a lot of money.

TOM: Why (4) .......................................... the money?

ALEX: I wanted to travel a bit before I started studying.

TOM: Where (5) .......................................... to go?

ALEX: Well, the Middle East, Latin America, Australia …

TOM: Wow! And (6) .......................................... all those places?

ALEX: No, not yet. I've been to Brazil and Peru so far. And I spent some months in Turkey.

TOM: Where (7) .......................................... there?

ALEX: With some friends near Izmir. It was great.

TOM: You're very lucky. And now you want to come to college.
(8) .......................................... some work to show me?

ALEX: Um, yes, I've got some paintings here.

TOM: Where (9) .......................................... these?

ALEX: Mostly in Turkey.

TOM: (10) .......................................... anything in South America?

ALEX: No, I didn't have time really. And I was travelling light, so I just did some pencil sketches. They're behind the paintings.

TOM: Well, Alex, I'm very impressed. When (11) .......................................... interested in painting and drawing?

ALEX: I think I always have been.

TOM: I can believe that. This work is very good.

ALEX: Thank you very much.

**42** Choose ten of the pictures and write true sentences about yourself. Use the present perfect or past simple.

| | | | | |
|---|---|---|---|---|
| do / washing up | drive / car | eat / noodles | wear / hat | ride / motorbike |
| get / married | play / computer game | play / golf | pass / exam | break / leg |
| watch / TV | ride / bike | study / English | drink / milk | text / my best friend |

**1** I ...*haven't played a computer game*............................................................... since last month.

**2** Yesterday I ......................................................................................................................... .

**3** In the past six months I ...................................................................................................... .

**4** Since my last birthday I ..................................................................................................... .

**5** I ............................................................................................................................ recently.

**6** Last year I .......................................................................................................................... .

**7** Six months ago I ................................................................................................................ .

**8** I ................................................................................................................ since I was a child.

**9** I .............................................................................................................. yesterday evening.

**10** This week I ........................................................................................................................ .

# Past simple, past continuous and past perfect

(I did, I was doing and I had done / I had been doing)

**43** Choose the correct alternative.

---

From:     Nonna@zapnet.com

To:       GHL@zapnet.com

Cc:       Margo35@kwikmail.co.uk

Subject: INTERNATIONAL STUDENT CONFERENCE

Hi!

Thought you'd like to know that the conference was very successful. 😊 The talks
(1) <u>were / had been</u> really interesting and all the speakers (2) <u>had prepared / prepared</u>
their material very thoroughly. Everyone agreed we should do the same next year.

However there were some problems with the conference centre. 😞 When we
(3) <u>arrived / had arrived</u>, we (4) <u>discovered / had discovered</u> that the manager
(5) <u>reserved / had reserved</u> the wrong room for us. This meant that we (6) <u>didn't have /
hadn't had</u> enough space. Unfortunately, he couldn't let us have the larger room because
he (7) <u>gave / had given</u> it to another group, which was even bigger than ours. 😞😞

He (8) <u>also misunderstood / had also misunderstood</u> the letter explaining what food
we (9) <u>wanted / had wanted</u>. In fact, we (10) <u>suspected / had suspected</u> that he
(11) <u>lost / had lost</u> it. I don't recommend using that place again!

CU
Nonna

---

**44** There are mistakes in all of these sentences. Correct the sentences.

1 I was pleased to see my friends from uni at the conference
last week <u>as we didn't see each other</u> since graduation.                    _as we hadn't seen each other_

2 By the time we reached the stadium, the match ended and
the spectators were leaving.                                                    ......................................................

3 At the end of the meal, he found he couldn't pay his
share of the bill because he didn't bring his wallet with him.                  ......................................................

4 We were pleased that Gary was having his laptop with him,
but we were less pleased when we discovered that he hadn't
charged the battery.                                                            ......................................................

5 When I came out of the cinema, I had found that a thief
had taken my phone from my bag.                                                 ......................................................

6 At first the authorities thought the athlete had been using
drugs, but they soon realised the lab mixed up the test results.               ......................................................

7 When my cousin came into the room, I didn't recognise him
because I didn't see him since he was at primary school.                       ......................................................

8 We couldn't find anywhere central to stay when we arrived
in Rome, so we had decided to book a hotel room the next time.                 ......................................................

*English Grammar in Use Supplementary Exercises*        **27**

**45** Complete the sentences with suitable verbs in the correct form: past perfect simple or past perfect continuous.

1. Why did Vicki have a shower?
   Because she'd been working out.
   VICKI

2. Why did Becca give you flowers?
   Because she ..................
   BECCA

3. Why didn't Jordan answer the door?
   Because he ..................
   JORDAN

4. Why didn't Simon arrive for his interview?
   Because he ..................
   SIMON

5. Why didn't Alex eat any lunch?
   Because he ..................
   ALEX

6. Why did Cora miss the bus?
   Because she ..................
   CORA

7. Why didn't Ellie go to the beach?
   Because she ..................
   ELLIE

8. Why did Chris lose his job?
   Because he ..................
   CHRIS

**46** **Put the verbs into the correct form: past simple, past continuous, past perfect simple or past perfect continuous.**

Kylie has called to see her boyfriend Gary. They are both angry.

GARY: Kylie, I'm surprised to see you.

KYLIE: Yeah? Well, I think you owe me an explanation.

GARY: What about you? (1) ....I saw.... (I / see) you in the cafe last night.

(2) ................................................ (We / arrange) to meet at the cinema, if you remember.

KYLIE: So why (3) ................................................ (you / not / come) into the cafe if you saw me?

GARY: (4) ................................................ (I / be) too angry. And cold.

(5) ................................................ (I / wait) outside the cinema for three-quarters of an hour.

KYLIE: But why? (6) ................................................ (you / not / get) my text?

GARY: What text?

KYLIE: The text (7) ................................................ (I / send) you yesterday afternoon.

GARY: What are you taking about?

KYLIE: (8) ................................................ (I / walk) past the cinema yesterday lunchtime when

(9) ................................................ (I / notice) that (10) ................................................

(they / change) the movie. So (11) ................................................ (I / text) you to tell you.

GARY: (12) ................................................ (I / not / get) any texts from you yesterday.

KYLIE: What? Let me look at your phone. Yes, it's here.

GARY: Oh, no! Of course, my phone wasn't charged yesterday. I'm so sorry I was angry. It's just that,

well, while (13) ................................................ (I / wait), (14) ................................................

(I / worry) about (15) ................................................ (what / happen) to you. Then

(16) ................................................ (I / see) you in the cafe.

(17) ................................................ (You / laugh) with your friends and

(18) ................................................ (I / realise) that (19) ................................................

(you / sit) there in the warm with them all evening. That's why

(20) ................................................ (I / lose) my temper.

KYLIE: Never mind. Let's forget it. Where shall we go now?

GARY: What's on at the cinema, then?

KYLIE: A new musical. (21) ................................................ (My sister / see) it at the weekend.

(22) ................................................ (She / sing) the theme song all day yesterday.

GARY: Oh, you must be tired of hearing it.

KYLIE: I am. Let's just go and have something to eat, shall we?

GARY: Yes, that's a good idea.

# Past simple, past continuous and used to

(**I did**, **I was doing** and **I used to do**)

**47** Write sentences with **used to** or **didn't use to** and the verbs provided.

1 I had a yacht, but I sold it when my business failed. (own)
   <u>I used to own a yacht.</u>

2 I often eat olives now, although I wasn't keen on them when I was younger. (like)

3 I seem to have lost interest in meeting new people. (enjoy)

4 My sister has started visiting art galleries since moving to Paris. (be interested)

5 Now that I'm married, I have less time for football. (play)

6 My brother had his hair cut short when he left college. (have)

7 I didn't really see my uncle until he bought a house near ours. (live)

8 My husband had a job in Beijing before we lived here. (work)

9 I retired from the university five years ago. (teach)

10 We've bought bikes since we moved to the countryside. (cycle)

**48** Choose the correct alternative.

It is sometimes said that there is nothing new in the world of fashion. Annabelle was a well-known model during the seventies. When her granddaughter Zoe was a schoolchild, she (1) ~~was enjoying~~ / used to enjoy looking at granny's old photo albums. She (2) <u>was finding / found</u> it hard to believe that granny (3) <u>was wearing / used to wear</u> such strange clothes. (4) <u>Did people really use to think / Were people really thinking</u> flared trousers looked good? And those ugly platform shoes! Annabelle (5) <u>was admitting / admitted</u> that people (6) <u>were often falling / often used to fall</u> over because their heels were so high.

When Zoe went to university, however, Annabelle noticed to her amusement that seventies styles (7) <u>were / used to be</u> in fashion again. 'I (8) <u>planned / was planning</u> to throw all my old clothes away,' she said, 'but Zoe went to a party last week, and guess what she (9) <u>used to wear / was wearing</u> – that's right, some of my old clothes!'

**49** Underline the verbs which can be changed to **used to** (used to work / used to play / used to be, etc.) instead of the past simple. If no change is possible, write 'No change'. Rewrite the sentences with **used to** where possible.

1 In the winter vacation, Dan <u>worked</u> in a cafe while his friends were skiing.
   *In the winter vacation, Dan used to work in a cafe while his friends were skiing.*

2 Bruce cycled from Naples to Athens last summer, stopping each night in a different town.
   *No change*

3 My girlfriend had a favourite handbag which she had bought with her first wages.

4 As Lynda was getting out of the boat, her foot slipped and she fell into the river.

5 Before the new shopping centre was built, there was a football stadium here.

6 Jasper complained that the street wasn't full of litter until the fast food restaurant opened.

7 During our cruise I took several photos of the seabirds which followed the ship.

8 While I was waiting for the bus, I noticed a group of tourists who were listening to a guide.

9 The music in this club was very boring before they installed a new sound system.

10 I spent a lot of time helping with the housework when I was a kid, but my sister didn't help at all.

11 The politicians made lots of promises before the election but kept none of them, as usual.

**50** Write true sentences about yourself with **used to** or **didn't use to** and the words from the box.

| cinema | friends | grandparents | homework |
| jeans | music | restaurants | television |

1 *I used to go on holiday with my parents, but now I go with my friends.*
2 *I didn't use to wear jeans when I was a child.*
3
4
5
6
7
8

**51** Complete the sentences with suitable verbs in the correct form: past simple, past continuous or **used to**.

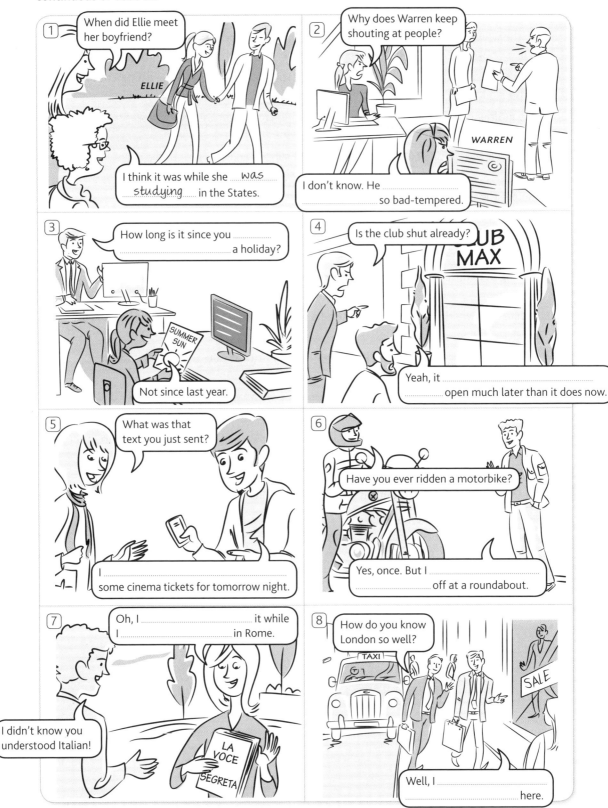

1. When did Ellie meet her boyfriend?

ELLIE

I think it was while she ....was studying.... in the States.

2. Why does Warren keep shouting at people?

WARREN

I don't know. He .................................... so bad-tempered.

3. How long is it since you .................... .................................... a holiday?

SUMMER SUN

Not since last year.

4. Is the club shut already?

CLUB MAX

Yeah, it .................................... .................... open much later than it does now.

5. What was that text you just sent?

I .................................... some cinema tickets for tomorrow night.

6. Have you ever ridden a motorbike?

Yes, once. But I .................................... .................... off at a roundabout.

7. Oh, I .................................... it while I .................................... in Rome.

I didn't know you understood Italian!

LA VOCE SEGRETA

8. How do you know London so well?

TAXI

SALE

Well, I .................................... .................................... here.

# Present, present perfect and past

**52** Choose the correct alternative.

**A** PETE: Whereabouts in Brighton (1) ~~do you live~~ / did you live / ~~have you lived~~ when
(2) you were / you've been / you were being a child?

PATRICK: The part called Kemp Town. (3) Do you know / Did you know / Have you known it?

PETE: Oh, yes. (4) I was eating / I used to eat / I've eaten there most weekends when
(5) I was doing / I've been doing / I've done my degree at the university.

**B** HELEN: When (6) are you hearing / did you hear / have you heard the result of your law exam?

CLARA: When (7) I phoned / I've phoned / I'd phoned my boss. (8) She's checking / She's been
checking / She was checking the results online when (9) I'd rung / I rang / I was ringing, so
(10) she's told / she was telling / she told me then.

HELEN: (11) Do you expect / Have you expected / Had you been expecting to do so well?

CLARA: Not really, to be honest!

HELEN: (12) Are you texting / Do you text / Have you texted your husband yet?

CLARA: Not yet.

HELEN: Go on! (13) He waited / He's waited / He's been waiting to hear from you all day.

**53** Put the verbs into the correct form: present simple, present continuous, past simple, past
continuous, present perfect simple, present perfect continuous or past perfect simple.

1 Tom has started training regularly since he ...*joined*... (join) the gym.

2 How often ........................................ (you / visit) your cousins when
........................................ (you / be) in Singapore last year?

3 I ........................................ (not top up) my phone credit yet. How much
........................................ (you / think) I need for a month?

4 The filling station manager called the police when he ........................................ (realise)
that someone ........................................ (drive) off without paying for their petrol.

5 Sharon's health ........................................ (seem) much better these days than it
used to be. Perhaps she ........................................ (take) vitamins as the doctor
........................................ (advise).

6 Eddie ........................................ (set) fire to his kitchen last week when he
........................................ (fry) sausages. He ........................................
(sort out) the mess ever since, as you can imagine.

7 My grandmother was a wonderful woman. She ........................................ (spend)
most of her life teaching adults who ........................................ (miss) the
opportunity to go to school when they ........................................ (be) children.

8 I ........................................ (always / want) to visit Japan.
Now that I ........................................ (have) the chance,
I ........................................ (decide) to take it.

9 We ........................................ (arrive) at the music festival on Friday afternoon, but a
lot of people ........................................ (get) there in the morning and the queue for
tickets ........................................ (be) already long.

10 My sister's in Vietnam at the moment. She ........................................ (have) such a
great time she ........................................ (want) to stay another six months.

# The future: present tenses and will/shall

(**I do / I am doing** and **I will/shall do**)

**54** Choose the correct alternative.

**A** BEN: Are you busy at the moment, Sam?

SAM: Yes. (1) ~~I prepare~~ / I'm preparing for a conference next Wednesday, but (2) that only lasts / that is only lasting until Friday so I'm free after that.

**B** PAT: Oh dear, I've spilt my coffee.

ALAN: Don't worry! (3) I get / I'll get a cloth.

**C** WILL: What time (4) does your evening class finish / is your evening class finishing?

LIZ: Half past nine.

WILL: (5) Shall I come / Do I come and collect you?

LIZ: Thanks, but (6) I meet / I'm meeting my sister for a drink.

**D** MIKE: Mum, (7) will you talk / are you talking to Dad for me?

MUM: What's the problem?

MIKE: Last week he said I could use the car at the weekend, but now (8) he doesn't let / he won't let me after all. I need it to get to the match (9) I play / I'm playing on Sunday.

MUM: OK. (10) I try / I'll try to make him change his mind. I expect (11) he's agreeing / he'll agree when I explain.

**55** Complete the email with the verbs from the box in the correct form: present simple, present continuous or will.

> be    do    ~~go~~    include    let    see    work

⊖ ◯ ◯

Hi Milo

I've had an idea about next year's holiday. I (1) _'m going_ to the Far East on a tour, starting on 10th July. Would you like to come too?

I know you (2) _____ in Moscow next summer, but I'm sure your company (3) _____ you fly to the Far East instead of coming back to Europe.

The tour (4) _____ ancient sites in Vietnam, Cambodia and Malaysia. There (5) _____ chances to take a break and relax too. Have a look at their website www.tourfarther.com and let me know what you think quickly because I (6) _____ the travel agent on Monday. I hope we (7) _____ this tour together.

All the best
Pedro

**56** Put the verbs into the correct form: present simple, present continuous or the **will/shall** future.

Gina and Mickey are going to an international students' conference. Gina's checking with Mickey about the arrangements he's made for them.

GINA: Is everything arranged for tomorrow? What time (1) ....*does our plane leave*.....
(our plane / leave)?

MICKEY: At seven-thirty, so (2) ................................................ (I / collect) you from your house at five.

GINA: Five! (3) ................................................ (I / have to) get up in the middle of the night.

MICKEY: I'm sorry, but we must check in by six and I think (4) ................................................
(there / probably / be) a long queue.

GINA: Oh, OK. What about the other end?

MICKEY: Well, (5) ................................................ (a local student / come) to the airport to meet us. He texted me this morning.

GINA: That's good. (6) ................................................ (We / be able to) talk to him on the way to the hostel.

MICKEY: Right. I believe (7) ................................................ (the conference / not start) until late afternoon. Anyway, (8) ................................................ (they / email) the programme to us before we leave.

GINA: Great. (9) ................................................ (I / read) it on the plane, I expect. Now, I'd better go and pack.

MICKEY: Yeah, me too. See you tomorrow at six.

GINA: Oh, yeah. I hope (10) ................................................ (I / be) awake.

MICKEY: So do I.

**57** Complete the following sentences about yourself using the words in brackets.

**1** This lesson ....*ends at twelve o'clock*............................................... . (end)
**2** At the weekend ...*I'll probably go to the cinema*.......................... . (probably go)
**3** Next summer ................................................................................. . (visit)
**4** When I finish this exercise, .......................................................... . (be)
**5** Tomorrow evening I expect .......................................................... . (eat)
**6** At the end of my course ............................................................... . (probably speak)
**7** My next class ............................................................................... . (begin)
**8** Next week ..................................................................................... . (have)
**9** My course ..................................................................................... . (finish)

**58** Imagine that you are in the following situations. Write what you say using **will**, **shall** or **won't**.

1

YOU

You offer to help her.
You say: I'll take the briefcase for you.
or Shall I carry something?

2

YOU

Don't be late.

You promise not to be late.
You say: ...........................................................

3

Can you deliver
before the weekend?

YOU

You agree to deliver the goods on Friday.
You say: ...........................................................

4

YOU

We haven't got
anything to do.

You suggest going to the swimming pool.
You say: ...........................................................

5

YOU

You ask them to stop fighting.
You say: ...........................................................

6

YOU

You explain the problem with the door.
You say: ...........................................................

7

YOU

You offer to phone for an ambulance.
You say: ...........................................................

8

YOU

You refuse to pay for the goods until you've
checked that they aren't damaged.
You say: ...........................................................
...........................................................

# The future: present continuous, will/shall, going to

(**I am doing**, **I will/shall do** and **I am going to do**)

**59** Write sentences with **going to** and the words in brackets.

**1** It's Rowland's birthday next week. (send him a card)
*I'm going to send him a card*

**2** Look at those dark clouds. (rain very soon)

**3** John forgot his Mum's birthday. (be in trouble)

**4** This room is a mess. (who / help me tidy up?)

**5** Alex and Tony can't afford to stay in a hotel. (buy a tent)

**6** This music is boring. (not come to this club again)

**7** I need to get more exercise. (walk to work from now on)

**8** I'm very tired this morning. (have another coffee)

**9** We haven't got any money. (how / get home?)

**10** I need to leave home very early tomorrow. (buy petrol tonight)

**11** My parents dislike flying. (travel to Prague by train)

**12** Leila's lost her phone. (contact her?)

**60** Choose the correct alternative.

**1** The sports club has put up the prices again. ~~I'll cancel~~ / I'm going to cancel my membership.
**2** I've talked to my boss, but he's very unhelpful and won't do / isn't going to do anything about the problem.
**3** I'll go / I'm going to go into town this afternoon. Can I get you anything?
**4** Will you hold / Are you going to hold this box for a moment while I unpack it?
**5** I hear the government's announced they'll raise / they're going to raise taxes again.
**6** My car won't start / isn't going to start. It must be the cold, I think.
**7** I'll start / I'm going to start a new job next week.
**8** I'm so sorry I forgot your birthday. Why don't you come round tomorrow evening and I'll cook / I'm going to cook you a meal?
**9** I took these trousers back to the shop, but they won't change / aren't going to change them without a receipt.
**10** You look tired. Shall we eat / Are we going to eat early this evening?
**11** John's sold his car. He'll buy / He's going to buy a bike, he says.
**12** I've decided what to do for my holiday. I'll go / I'm going to go to Morocco.

**61** Put the verbs into the correct form: the **will/shall** future or the **going to** future.

Mary and Nigel run a sportswear shop together. They are having money problems.

**Monday**

MARY: I don't know what (1) ....*we're going to do*.... (we / do). We've hardly made any money for ages.

NIGEL: I think we should advertise. We can send out leaflets.

MARY: Yes. (2) ....*That'll probably get*.... (That / probably / get) the shop more widely known. But do you think (3) ........................................ (people / come) here?

NIGEL: Well, we could try to get more online sales.

MARY: Yes, we need to improve our website. (4) ........................................ (I / phone) the designer. And what about advertising on local radio?

NIGEL: Good idea. (5) ........................................ (I / phone) them?

MARY: OK, thanks.

**Tuesday**

MARY: We haven't got enough money to pay for radio advertising and updating the website. I've been in touch with the bank. (6) ........................................ (I / see) a business advisor called William there on Friday.

NIGEL: (7) ........................................ (he / help) us to get a loan, do you think?

MARY: I hope so.

**Friday**

WILLIAM: So you want to borrow some money. How do you want to spend it?

MARY: (8) ........................................ (We / advertise) on the radio and update our website. We've planned it carefully. We only need £5,000.

WILLIAM: OK. (9) ........................................ (The bank / lend) you the money. But you must pay us back in three months. Can you do that?

MARY: (10) ........................................ (We / do) it, I promise.

WILLIAM: Now, I just need a few more details, then (11) ........................................ (I / help) you fill in the necessary forms.

MARY: Thank you.

WILLIAM: You're welcome.

**62**  **Complete the conversations. Use will/shall, going to or the present continuous.**

**A** ANN:  It just said on the radio that (1) ___*it's going to snow*___ .

BILL:  Oh, did it? I (2) ___*'ll take*___ my big coat then.

JOE:  Good idea. So (3) ....................................................................... . Come on, Bill. Let's go.

**B** ED:  Jenny's had her baby.

GAIL:  Really? That's wonderful! (4) ................................................................ her some flowers.

ED:  (5) ................................................................ her this afternoon at the hospital.

(6) ................................................................ them to her for you if you want.

GAIL:  (7) ................................................................ you? Thanks very much. In that case,

(8) ................................................................ and buy them right away.

**C** KEN:  I haven't got a clean shirt. (9) ................................................................ one for me?

LILY:  No, (10) ................................................................ . You can do your own washing!

**63**  **Write what you would say in these situations. Use will/shall, going to or the present continuous.**

**1** You make your friend a cup of sweet coffee, then she tells you she doesn't take sugar.
Offer to make her another one.
You: ___I'm sorry, I'll make you another one___

**2** A colleague asks why you're leaving work early. Explain that you have arranged to meet your grandmother at the airport.
You: ................................................................................................................................

**3** Your brother lent you some money last week. Promise to pay him back at the weekend.
You: ................................................................................................................................

**4** Your sister has bought some clothes from a cheap website. You want to buy some too and you've asked her several times for the address, but she refuses to tell you. Ask why she refuses to tell you.
You: ...........................................................................................................................?

**5** You failed an exam last year. Since then you've been working hard. Tell your teacher it's because you're determined not to fail again.
You: ................................................................................................................................

**6** Your neighbour is playing loud music late at night. You get angry and ask him to turn the volume down.
You: ...........................................................................................................................?

**7** You've been offered a role in a film and have accepted. Tell your friends about it.
You: ...........................................................................................................................!

**8** A friend is telling you about a travel scholarship she has won. Ask her which countries she plans to visit.
You: ................................................................................................................................

# The future: all forms

**64** Put the verbs into the correct form: **present simple, present continuous, the will/shall future, the going to future, the future continuous or the future perfect.**

**A** Mick is watching television when his sister Vanessa comes into the room.

MICK: What are you doing in your dressing-gown? It's only eight o'clock.

VANESSA: I don't feel well. (1) _I'm going to have_ (I / have) an early night.

MICK: Bad luck. I hope (2) _you feel_ (you / feel) better in the morning.

VANESSA: So do I. (3) _____ (I / meet) my new boss at ten o'clock.

MICK: I think (4) _____ (I / make) some tea when this programme (5) _____ (finish). (6) _____ (I / bring) you a cup?

VANESSA: No, don't bother. (7) _____ (I / try) and go straight to sleep. Thanks anyway.

MICK: OK. Sleep well.

**B** Sandy and Alison are students who have been sharing a flat. Sandy is leaving to do a course in the USA.

SANDY: It's hard saying goodbye after so long.

ALISON: Yeah. Remember to send me your phone number when (8) _____ (you / get) your new phone in the States. And you've promised to Skype® me.

SANDY: Yeah, we can do that a lot. But (9) _____ (I / probably / not / have) time the first few days because (10) _____ (my course / start) as soon as (11) _____ (I / arrive), and (12) _____ (I / spend) the weekend with some friends of my father's.

ALISON: I know, of course.

SANDY: Anyway, do you know what (13) _____ (you / do) this time the Sunday after next?

ALISON: (14) _____ (I / get) ready to go to London.

SANDY: OK. So, (15) _____ (I / Skype) you about three o'clock that Sunday afternoon.

ALISON: Great.

# Can, could and be able to

**65** Choose the correct alternative.

1 Why did you walk from the station? You ~~could phone~~ / could have phoned me for a lift.

2 I loved staying with my grandparents when I was a child. They let me read all their books and told me I could go / was able to go to bed as late as I wanted.

3 This carpet was priced at £500, but I could get / was able to get a discount because of this little mark in the corner.

4 I couldn't have found / haven't been able to find my mobile for days. It's making my life impossible!

5 I've no idea where my brother is now. He can be / could be at the North Pole for all I know.

6 It's hard to imagine how scientists cope with the Antarctic climate. I'm sure I can't / couldn't.

7 We could cook / could have cooked in our holiday flat, but we preferred to eat out.

**66** Tick (✓) the best sentence in each pair, or tick both if both are possible.

1 *a* I broke my new necklace but luckily my sister could fix it for me. ✗
  *b* I broke my new necklace but luckily my sister was able to fix it for me. ✓

2 *a* Emily was with Tom when her phone was stolen, so she could use his to call me.
  *b* Emily was with Tom when her phone was stolen, so she was able to use his to call me.

3 *a* I didn't enjoy the match because I forgot my glasses. I couldn't see the ball.
  *b* I didn't enjoy the match because I forgot my glasses. I wasn't able to see the ball.

4 *a* In the end, Marion could come with us because her meeting was cancelled.
  *b* In the end, Marion was able to come with us because her meeting was cancelled.

5 *a* Bob couldn't speak Dutch when he arrived in Holland, but he's almost fluent now.
  *b* Bob wasn't able to speak Dutch when he arrived in Holland, but he's almost fluent now.

6 *a* I'd planned to get a taxi after the party, but luckily I could have a lift with Kate.
  *b* I'd planned to get a taxi after the party, but luckily I was able to have a lift with Kate.

7 *a* We really wanted to buy a new car last year, but we just couldn't afford it.
  *b* We really wanted to buy a new car last year, but we just weren't able to afford it.

8 *a* My brother could read well by the age of seven, but he had problems with maths.
  *b* My brother was able to read well by the age of seven, but he had problems with maths.

9 *a* Last night we heard a noise outside our window and when we turned off the light inside, we could see a fox by the rubbish bin.
  *b* Last night we heard a noise outside our window and when we turned off the light inside, we were able to see a fox by the rubbish bin.

10 *a* One day last week I locked my sister out of the house by mistake, but luckily she could get in through an open window!
  *b* One day last week I locked my sister out of the house by mistake, but luckily she was able to get in through an open window!

# May and might

**67** Answer the questions with **might** or **might have** and the ideas in brackets.

**1** What flavour ice cream shall we buy for Liz, vanilla or strawberry?
(prefer chocolate) *She might prefer chocolate.*

**2** Why is Alan in such a bad mood today?
(sleep badly last night) *He might have slept badly last night.*

**3** Why didn't Jane come to the party with her boyfriend last night?
(have a row) ........................................................................................

**4** Why is Anna looking under the desk?
(drop something) ........................................................................................

**5** I can't remember where I put my bag. Do you?
(be under the bed) ........................................................................................

**6** Why hasn't anybody said 'Happy Birthday' to me?
(plan a surprise) ........................................................................................

**7** Why does Henry look so miserable?
(have some bad news) ........................................................................................

**8** Why isn't Sophie in the office today?
(work at home) ........................................................................................

**9** Why didn't Rosemary come to the cinema last night?
(have something better to do) ........................................................................................

**68** Use **might** to complete the sentences which explain why you should follow this advice.

**1** You should reserve a seat on the train for long journeys.
If you don't, *you might have to stand all the way* .

**2** You'd better not leave your laptop in the garden.
If you do, *someone might steal it* .

**3** You should use a SatNav when you drive in London.
If you don't, ........................................................................................ .

**4** You should allow plenty of time to go through security checks at the airport.
If you don't, ........................................................................................ .

**5** You ought not to eat too much fast food.
If you do, ........................................................................................ .

**6** You'd better revise thoroughly before your exam.
If you don't, ........................................................................................ .

**7** You should have your car serviced regularly.
If you don't, ........................................................................................ .

**8** You shouldn't go clubbing the night before you start a new job.
If you do, ........................................................................................ .

**9** You ought to arrive punctually for meetings with your boss.
If you don't, ........................................................................................ .

**10** You shouldn't shout at your brother.
If you do, ........................................................................................ .

# Can, could, may, might, must and can't

**69** Match the beginning of each sentence with the most suitable ending.

| | | |
|---|---|---|
| 1 You must have met some fascinating people | a after all your hard work. | 1 _d_ |
| 2 You must know Tokyo is expensive | b after touring the world for years. | 2 |
| 3 You can't have lived in Tunisia for ten years | c if you've lived there. | 3 |
| 4 You can't be tired | d during your trip to Africa. | 4 |
| 5 You must be exhausted | e when you've just had a holiday. | 5 |
| 6 You may find it difficult to settle down | f without learning some Arabic. | 6 |
| 7 You couldn't have gone on holiday | g to the airport tomorrow. | 7 |
| 8 You might think about going to Spain | h because you had no money. | 8 |
| 9 You could take a taxi | i for your next holiday. | 9 |

**70** Complete the email with the words from the box.

> may be seeing    may not have done    could have fallen
> ~~may have left~~    couldn't have left    may be visiting
> could be coming    may have found

**From:** Robin Nicholas

**To:** Helena Shakespeare

**Subject:** Seeing you again

Hi Helena,

It was good to see you last week and show you our research facilities here. Thanks for your email. Sorry to hear you lost your iPod on the journey home. I've looked for it, but it definitely isn't in our office. I think you (1) _may have left_ it on the train. Why not phone the lost property office? It (2) ............................................ down the side of your seat. Someone (3) ............................................ it and handed it in. Of course, if they like music, they (4) ............................................ ! Anyway, as far as I remember, you (5) ............................................ it here, because you were listening to it on the way to the station.

And now my news. Guess what? I (6) ............................................ to your part of the world next month for a conference! My professor wanted to attend it, but now he's heard that some important scientists (7) ............................................ our laboratory at that time. So, you and I (8) ............................................ each other sooner than we expected. I'll email as soon as I know for certain.

All the best,
Robin

**71** Choose the correct alternative.

1 You <u>must be</u> / ~~can't be~~ very proud of your daughter winning the race.

2 I expected my boyfriend to call after work last night, but he didn't. I suppose he <u>must be</u> / <u>must have been</u> too tired.

3 That group is so famous now, it <u>must be</u> / <u>can't be</u> easy to get tickets to see them perform.

4 I'm sure we can get online here if we try. We <u>must be using</u> / <u>can't be using</u> the right password.

5 I've just rung the garage to check whether they've fixed my car, but I can't get an answer. I suppose they <u>may have</u> / <u>may be having</u> a break in the yard.

6 I don't know why you wanted to stay at that party. You <u>might have enjoyed</u> / <u>can't have enjoyed</u> talking to all those boring people.

7 I can't go out this morning. We're getting a new TV and the store <u>may be delivering</u> / <u>must be delivering</u> it today.

8 Please check these figures again. They're not accurate. You <u>might have been concentrating</u> / <u>can't have been concentrating</u> when you added them up.

9 You <u>must be</u> / <u>must have been</u> thirsty after playing tennis all afternoon. Shall I get you a drink?

**72** Complete the answers with **must**, **can't** or **might** and any other words you need.

1 GERALD: Can that be James phoning at this hour? It's gone midnight!

  HILDA: It _____might be_____ him. He said he'd phone if he passed his exam.

2 JIM: There's a light on in that office block. Do you think it's a thief?

  HARRY: It _____must be_____ the cleaners. They always work at night.

3 WILL: What are we having for Sunday dinner?

  TESSA: It _____ chicken. Mum often does chicken on Sundays.

4 CLARE: Is that your daughter's coat?

  FIONA: No, it _____ hers. It's much too big.

5 ANDY: Where did I put my trainers? I can't remember.

  JANE: They _____ the car. You often leave them there.

6 ELINOR: Where did Adam get that new guitar? He hasn't got any money.

  KATE: It _____ a present. After all, it was his birthday last week.

7 NICKY: Why did Mina ignore me at the party last night?

  RYAN: She _____ you. She wasn't wearing her glasses.

8 EMMA: Do you think Cindy told the boss I left work early yesterday?

  NEIL: She's away this week, so she _____ him.

9 JILL: What's making me feel so ill?

  PAT: It _____ ate. Did you have seafood last night? That sometimes makes people ill.

# Must(n't), need(n't), should(n't) and don't have to

**73** Match the beginning of each sentence with the most suitable ending.

1 Lucy should be having breakfast,

2 Patsy shouldn't go clubbing all night

3 Jenny shouldn't have gone out

4 Megan mustn't oversleep

5 Nicky doesn't have to get up yet

6 Natalie didn't need to hurry

7 Sharon needn't have set the alarm clock

a when she was supposed to be studying.

b because she woke up early anyway.

c ~~but she's too nervous to eat.~~

d when she has an exam the next day.

e if she's not going to work today.

f or she'll be late for her interview.

g because she wasn't late.

1 ....c....

2 ................

3 ................

4 ................

5 ................

6 ................

7 ................

**74** Choose the correct alternative.

**Thursday**

NEIL: We're doing our presentation to the seminar group next Monday. Can you email them right away?

ROBBIE: (1) Must I do / ~~Should I do~~ it now?

NEIL: Well, we (2) must have told / should have told them earlier really.

ROBBIE: Oh, all right then.

**Friday**

NAOMI: I've had an email about Neil and Robbie's presentation on Monday.

ELLIE: That's strange, I haven't. Do you think I (3) must / ought to call them?

NAOMI: No, you (4) mustn't / don't have to. It's probably not relevant to your research area.

**Monday**

NAOMI: Hi, Neil. I've come a bit early in case you wanted help to get the room ready. But I see I (5) needn't bother / needn't have bothered, you've got everything organised!

NEIL: Isn't Ellie with you?

NAOMI: No, she didn't get an email from you, so we thought the presentation wasn't relevant to her work.

NEIL: Oh, dear. Robbie (6) must send / must have sent the email to the wrong address.

NAOMI: Where he is now? He (7) must be / should be here.

NEIL: I don't know. He (8) must have forgotten / should have forgotten we're doing this presentation. He's so unreliable!

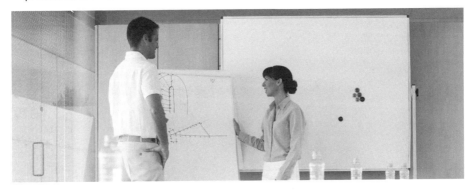

**75** For each pair of sentences, write *same* if sentences *a* and *b* have the same meaning. If the meaning is different, try to explain.

1 *a* It is vital to wear a helmet when you ride a motorbike.
   *b* You must wear a helmet when you ride a motorbike.                                    ...........same...........

2 *a* I expect we'll get the contract because we offered the best price.
   *b* We offered the best price, so we should get the contract.                            .................

3 *a* It isn't necessary for us to spend a long time in the museum if it's not interesting.
   *b* We shouldn't spend a long time in the museum if it's not interesting.                .................

4 *a* It was wrong of you to open the package.
   *b* You must have opened the package.                                                    .................

5 *a* She promised to phone me before lunch. It's seven o'clock now.
   *b* She should have phoned me by now.                                                    .................

6 *a* I made far more sandwiches than we needed.
   *b* I needn't make so many sandwiches.                                                   .................

7 *a* It's essential that my father doesn't find out what I've done.
   *b* My father must have found out what I've done.                                        .................

8 *a* In my opinion it would be wrong for them to move house now.
   *b* I don't think they need to move house now.                                           .................

9 *a* My sister offered me a lift, so it wasn't necessary for me to call a taxi.
   *b* As my sister offered me a lift, I didn't need to call a taxi.                        .................

10 *a* I think it's a good idea to check the timetable before we leave.
    *b* We should have checked the timetable before we left.                                .................

**76** Complete the sentences with **must(n't)**, **needn't** or **should(n't)**.

1 My phone's out of credit. I ........._must_......... top it up before I do anything else.

2 You ........................... finish that essay tonight if you're too tired. Midday tomorrow is the deadline.

3 What are you doing here? ........................... you be at college?

4 He really ........................... have told his brother about this present. It was supposed to be a secret.

5 You ........................... pay to go into this exhibition because I've got my membership card with me.

6 You ........................... make so much noise. We'll be asked to leave the restaurant if you don't stop shouting.

7 I'm going to be in trouble. I ........................... have texted my mum earlier this afternoon and I completely forgot.

8 You ........................... have gone to the bus station, you can book tickets online.

**77** Read the rules of the Fitness Centre. Complete what the instructor says with **must(n't)**, **need(n't)** or **should(n't)**.

## SPORTS CLUB NOTICE

• It is vital to have a health check before using the gym for the first time.

• It isn't necessary for members to pay for towels, but guests are charged £1 per towel.

• It is recommended that you begin with light exercises to warm up.

• It is not recommended that you exercise after a heavy meal.

• It's a good idea to ask a member of staff if you're not sure how to use the equipment.

• It is forbidden to use the Fitness Centre against the advice of the staff.

You (1) ...*must*... have a health check before using the gym for the first time.

You (2) .................... pay for towels, but your guests (3) .................... pay £1.

You (4) .................... begin with light exercises to warm up.

You (5) .................... exercise after a heavy meal.

You (6) .................... ask a member of staff if you're not sure how to use the equipment.

You (7) .................... use the Fitness Centre against the advice of the staff.

**78** Read what James did. Then complete what the instructor says with **must(n't)**, **need(n't)** or **should(n't)**.

James became a member of the Sports Club yesterday. He used the gym without having a health check. He paid for a towel. He didn't begin with light exercises. He exercised soon after eating a big lunch. He didn't ask a member of staff how to use the equipment. His back is very painful today.

James (1) .................... have used the gym without having a health check, so it's not my fault his back is very painful.

He (2) .................... have paid for a towel.

He (3) .................... have begun with light exercises.

He (4) .................... have exercised soon after lunch.

He (5) .................... have asked me how to use the equipment.

He (6) .................... have injured his back.

# (Don't) have to, should(n't), had better (not) and ought (not) to

Units 31, 33, 35

**79**  Read the situations and write sentences with **ought (not) to**. Some of the sentences are past and some are present.

1 Andy is very shy. His teacher chose him to make a speech to the whole school.
His teacher *ought not to have chosen Andy to make a speech to the whole school* .

2 Carla has an exam on Monday. She plans to spend the weekend at a music festival.
She ................................................................................................................................................ .

3 I live in Kyoto. You went there last week, but you didn't visit me.
You ................................................................................................................................................ .

4 Dan has a new MP3 player. His children used it without his permission.
They ............................................................................................................................................... .

5 You've bought a new phone. The shop said it had unlimited texts, but it has only ten a day.
They ............................................................................................................................................... .

6 We wanted to fly home at the weekend, but the flights were all full. We hadn't booked seats.
We ................................................................................................................................................. .

**80**  Tick (✓) the correct sentence in each pair, or tick both if both are correct.

1 *a* You should always lock your front door when you go out. ✓
*b* You'd better always lock your front door when you go out.

2 *a* I should leave now or I'll miss my bus.
*b* I'd better leave now or I'll miss my bus.

3 *a* I don't think people should keep pets if they don't have time to care for them properly.
*b* I don't think people had better keep pets if they don't have time to care for them properly.

4 *a* If you want to take photos here, you should ask permission or we might get into trouble.
*b* If you want to take photos here, you'd better ask permission or we might get into trouble.

5 *a* You should wear a coat. It's cold outside.
*b* You'd better wear a coat. It's cold outside.

6 *a* Would you mind getting stamps when you're out? The money I gave you should be enough.
*b* Would you mind getting stamps when you're out? The money I gave you had better be enough.

7 *a* I realise you must be surprised to see us. Perhaps I should explain what's going on.
*b* I realise you must be surprised to see us. Perhaps I'd better explain what's going on.

8 *a* People really should wear a helmet when they ride a bike.
*b* People really had better wear a helmet when they ride a bike.

9 *a* Passengers on long flights should move their legs as much as possible.
*b* Passengers on long flights had better move their legs as much as possible.

10 *a* Tell Jess that she should bring some cash if we're going out tonight.
*b* Tell Jess that she'd better bring some cash if we're going out tonight.

**81** Complete the email with **had better**, **should** or **have to**. Sometimes there is more than one answer.

---

**From:** Anna James.com
**To:** Gary Newlands
**Subject:** Travel tips

Gary,

I know you haven't done such a long flight before so I thought I (1) _'d better_ give you a few
tips. First, you (2) ................................................ make sure you get to the airport really early
because you always (3) ................................................ spend ages getting through security.
You (4) ................................................ be prepared for them to open all your hand
luggage too. Your flight is an early one so, with luck, you (5) ................................................
be able to get a seat in the business lounge. You (6) ................................................ (not)
pay for breakfast as it's free there. When your flight's called, you
(7) ................................................ start moving to the gate immediately because
sometimes you (8) ................................................ walk for about fifteen minutes.
You (9) ................................................ (not) take very heavy hand luggage because you
(10) ................................................ carry it yourself and you can't take a trolley to the gates.
Everyone agrees there (11) ................................................ be some, of course, but there
aren't. You get a meal on the flight of course, and you (12) ................................................ eat
it even if it doesn't taste very interesting, because there's nowhere to eat until you reach your hotel
at the other end. If you have any questions, email me.

Regards, Anna

---

**82** Complete the second sentence with **(don't) have to**, **should (not)** or **had better (not)** so that
it has a similar meaning to the first.

**1** It is compulsory to wear a helmet when you ride a motorbike.
You _have to wear a helmet when you ride a motorbike_ .

**2** It's advisable to check that all the windows are shut whenever you go out.
You ......................................................................................................................... .

**3** It's not acceptable to borrow money from people you hardly know.
You ......................................................................................................................... .

**4** I suggest we keep the door shut in case someone sees us.
You ......................................................................................................................... .

**5** Training regularly is essential if you want to succeed in athletics.
You ......................................................................................................................... .

**6** I don't think it's a good idea to take your phone to the beach. It might get stolen.
You ......................................................................................................................... .

**7** It'd be a good idea to change your shirt before the guests arrive.
You ......................................................................................................................... .

**8** There is no extra charge for delivery.
You ......................................................................................................................... .

# Should

**83** Tick (✓) the correct sentences.

**1** *a* After a match, the captain insists the football team should take things easy. ✓

*b* After a match, the captain insists the football team take things easy. ✓

*c* After a match, the captain insists the football team to take things easy.

**2** *a* The journalist demanded that the minister resigned.

*b* The journalist demanded that the minister resign.

*c* The journalist demanded that the minister should resign.

**3** *a* If you really want to get rich fast, I suggest you should work harder.

*b* If you really want to get rich fast, I suggest you work harder.

*c* If you really want to get rich fast, I suggest you to work harder.

**4** *a* He never has any money, so it's very odd that he have a new car.

*b* He never has any money, so it's very odd that he has a new car.

*c* He never has any money, so it's very odd that he should have a new car.

**5** *a* I think the weather will stay dry, but you can borrow my raincoat if by any chance it rains.

*b* I think the weather will stay dry, but you can borrow my raincoat if by any chance it should rain.

*c* I think the weather will stay dry, but you can borrow my raincoat if by any chance it rained.

**6** *a* My doctor explained that it was important I should take more exercise.

*b* My doctor explained that it was important I take more exercise.

*c* My doctor explained that it was important I took more exercise.

**84** There are mistakes in five of these sentences. Correct the sentences where necessary. Write 'OK' if the sentence is already correct.

**1** We were very surprised <u>that Tom behave</u> in such a rude manner.

that Tom behaved /
that Tom should behave

**2** I asked a friend about getting train tickets and he recommended to book online.

**3** The government accepted the recommendation that they reduce spending on the armed services.

**4** If I can't use a phone here, how do you suggest me to contact my offce?

**5** I shouldn't go in there if I were you. They're having an argument about money.

**6** Should be my phone off when you call, just leave a message on voicemail.

**7** It's essential that I should see the doctor today.

**8** Why didn't you demand the club to refund your subscription?

# Should

**85** Complete the conversation with **should** where necessary. Leave out **should** where possible.

BEN: We've got a review of the company's environmental footprint today and I can't find our latest energy consumption figures. What (1) ...*should I do*... (I / do)?

SUE: I really don't know. It's odd that (2) ........................................................ (the figures / disappear) just when you need them. Did you ask Rose?

BEN: Yes. She insisted that (3) ........................................................ (I / check) all the files myself.

SUE: She's so unhelpful.

BEN: And where's Jack? He promised to update me on new machinery costs.

SUE: I saw him printing off some figures a few minutes ago.

BEN: It's important (4) ........................................................ (we / discuss) his report before the meeting.

SUE: Shall I go and find him?

BEN: No, (5) ........................................................ (I / not / bother). He's probably on his way.

SUE: OK. Are you going to stay in the office over lunchtime?

BEN: Yes. It's vital (6) ........................................................ (I / find) these figures for this afternoon's meeting.

SUE: Oh, right. Well, I'm going out to give a talk to some new graduates about our industry this afternoon, so, if (7) ........................................................ (anyone / call), will you say I'm not available till tomorrow?

BEN: Are we going to recruit new staff?

SUE: Well, I'd like to, but the accountant's recommendation is that (8) ........................................................ (we / wait) until later in the year. He says we can't afford anyone yet. He suggests (9) ........................................................ (we / hire) someone temporary if we really have to.

BEN: I suppose it's only natural (10) ........................................................ (he / be) cautious. But we could really do with permanent help.

SUE: Yes, quite.

**86** Use your own ideas to complete the sentences.

1 In most countries motorcyclists must  *wear a helmet* .

2 I nearly missed the first class this morning. I should have .

3 I decided I didn't like the shoes I'd bought, but luckily I was able to .

4 The shops are always terribly crowded on Saturdays, so I may .

5 Politicians ought not to .

6 Some people dislike flying, so they might .

7 Most people pass the driving test first time, so it can't .

8 I don't know why my brother hasn't phoned. He may have .

9 If you really want to get fit, you should .

10 When the price of petrol rose sharply, many people had to .

11 Can you imagine travelling before the invention of railways? It must have .

12 Commuter trains are often overcrowded, and people aren't able to .

13 I could  when I was ten, but I couldn't

.

14 That girl looks as if she's lost. We'd better .

**87** Read this notice. Then complete the advice for people who are coming to your school or place of work.

### Information for newcomers to London Language Institute

- You shouldn't miss lessons.
- You should bring your laptop if you have one.
- You mustn't be late for class.
- You must switch your phone off during lessons.
- You needn't bring a dictionary.
- You don't have to take any exams.

### Information for newcomers to

1 You shouldn't .

2 You should .

3 You mustn't .

4 You must .

5 You needn't .

6 You don't have to .

# If I do and If I did

**88** Choose the correct alternative.

1 If <u>I miss</u> / ~~I'll miss~~ lunch, I'll get a sandwich later.

2 We'll have to leave without John if <u>he doesn't arrive / he won't arrive</u> soon.

3 They <u>won't refund / didn't refund</u> your money if you haven't kept your receipt.

4 Will you send me a text when <u>you reach / you'll reach</u> Mexico City?

5 If I make some coffee, <u>do you cut / will you cut</u> the cake?

6 <u>Did you work / Would you work</u> harder if you were better paid?

7 If you <u>don't complain / didn't complain</u> so much, you might be more popular.

8 <u>Weren't my friends / Wouldn't my friends be</u> envious if they could only see me now!

**89** Complete the sentences using words and phrases from the box.

> would it help    ~~will she say~~    will you do
> will it cost     would you buy     would you say

1 EVA:   I don't know what's happened to the bag I borrowed from Jo.

  SUE:   What ___will she say___ if you don't find it?

  EVA:   I suppose she'll be very annoyed.

2 TIM:   I'm thinking of applying to do my MSc abroad.

  ANN:   Really? What _____ if you do that?

  TIM:   About 10,000 Euros, I think.

3 MAY:   I don't know how I'm going to pay my rent this week.

  LEE:   So, _____ if I lent you some money?

  MAY:   Well, yes, of course. But I can't borrow from you.

  LEE:   Don't be silly. How much do you want?

4 PAUL:  I wish I could afford a new car.

  TINA:  What _____ if you could afford one?

  PAUL:  Oh, I wouldn't mind what it was – as long as it didn't keep breaking down.

5 BILL:  I don't think I'm going to pass my driving test next week.

  BEN:   What _____ if you don't?

  BILL:  I'll have to take it again. I need it to get the job I want.

6 JO:    Where's my bag? You know, the one I lent to you.

  EVA:   Oh. What _____ if I'd lost it?

  JO:    I'd tell you to get me a new one!

**90**　Put the verbs into the correct form.

**1** If I had more money, ....would you marry.... (you / marry) me?

**2** The teacher wouldn't help you if ........................................................... (he / not / like) you.

**3** ........................................................... (you / see) what the hotel looks like if you look at the website.

**4** ........................................................... (your boyfriend / not / be) amazed if he could see you now?

**5** If ........................................................... (I / not / revise) thoroughly, I may not get a good mark.

**6** If you wanted to buy your dad a present, what ........................................................... (you / look for)?

**7** Sally would have a lot more friends if ........................................................... (she / not / be) so mean.

**8** How ........................................................... (you / feel) if you were in my situation?

**9** Would you change your job if ........................................................... (you / can)?

**91**　Lisa and Trish are students. They're talking about what to do after university. Write sentences using the words given.

TRISH:　Do you have any plans for next year?

LISA:　Well, I don't have much money. But I speak Portuguese and Spanish. So (1) I / travel / if I / afford it.
　　　....I'd travel if I could afford it.

TRISH:　(2) If you / find / a job using your languages / you / take it?
　　　...........................................................

LISA:　(3) If it / be / in South America / I / certainly / consider it carefully.
　　　...........................................................

　　　I've always wanted to go there.

TRISH:　What about working as a tour guide, taking tourists round?
　　　(4) That / be / a great way to travel if you / speak the right languages.
　　　...........................................................

LISA:　But (5) I / only / consider / a job like that if I / be / sure the travel company was a good one.
　　　...........................................................

　　　(6) If the tourists / not / like / their hotels and so on, I / have a terrible time.
　　　...........................................................

TRISH:　Yes. (7) You / be / handling complaints every day if they / not / be / happy.
　　　...........................................................

LISA:　Exactly! (8) But if I / decide / to apply for a job like that, / you / help me with my application?
　　　...........................................................

TRISH:　Of course. And, I'm sure (9) you / succeed, if you / do.
　　　...........................................................

LISA:　Thanks very much.

**92**  Write questions using **if** for the following answers.

1   What would you do if someone gave            I'd probably give it to my mother.
    you a diamond necklace                 ?

2   ........................................    I'd share it with my friends.
    ...................................... ?

3   ........................................    I'd call the police.
    ...................................... ?

4   ........................................    We'd get out as fast as we could.
    ...................................... ?

5   ........................................    I'd ask my teacher's advice about it.
    ...................................... ?

6   ........................................    He'd be extremely angry.
    ...................................... ?

7   ........................................    She'd probably fall over.
    ...................................... ?

8   ........................................    I'd be late for work.
    ...................................... ?

9   ........................................    We'd sail around the world.
    ...................................... ?

10  ........................................    They'd never make any money.
    ...................................... ?

11  ........................................    There'd be no more wars.
    ...................................... ?

12  ........................................    I'd stay at home all day.
    ...................................... ?

**93**  Look at the questions you wrote for Exercise 92. Now write new answers of your own to
your questions.

1  What would you do if someone gave you a diamond necklace?
    I'd sell it and buy a horse. ..................................................

2  ........................................................................................
3  ........................................................................................
4  ........................................................................................
5  ........................................................................................
6  ........................................................................................
7  ........................................................................................
8  ........................................................................................
9  ........................................................................................
10 ........................................................................................
11 ........................................................................................
12 ........................................................................................

# If I did and If I had done

**94**  Match the beginning of each sentence with the most suitable ending.

| | | |
|---|---|---|
| **1** If you had been promoted, | *a* you'd be able to change the system. | 1 _____e_____ |
| **2** If you were rude to the boss, | *b* would you have left the firm? | 2 _____ |
| **3** If you were promoted, | *c* you wouldn't be sacked. | 3 _____ |
| **4** If you hadn't been promoted, | *d* you wouldn't get a reference. | 4 _____ |
| **5** If you had lost your job, | ~~*e* would you have made any changes?~~ | 5 _____ |
| **6** If you apologised, | *f* you'd probably regret it later. | 6 _____ |
| **7** If you were fired, | *g* you'd have been very upset. | 7 _____ |

**95**  Complete the conversations with suitable verbs.

**1** SEAN:  Why didn't you go to the lecture last night?

JIM:  I didn't know about it.

SEAN:  So __would you have gone__ if you __had known__ ?

**2** JILL:  Jane's got a PhD, hasn't she?

MILLY:  Yeah. I don't know why she works in this lab. I ..................................................
something worthwhile if I ................................................ her qualifications.

JILL:  What kind of work would you do?

MILLY:  Oh, I don't know exactly. But if I ................................................ Jane,
I ................................................ to do original research.

**3** SAM:  Why did you ask Veronica about her boyfriend? It really upset her.

MICK:  Well, I didn't realise they'd split up.

SAM:  You didn't know, then?

MICK:  Of course not. If I ................................................ ,
I ................................................ her about him.

**4** TIM:  Hey, I've got a text from Cheryl!

PAT:  Look out! Mind the step.

TIM:  Ouch! I've hurt my knee.

PAT:  Well, you ................................................ it if you
................................................ that text.

**5** JOHN:  Do you love me?

ROSE:  You know I do.

JOHN:  Would you ................................................ me if
I ................................................ poor?

ROSE:  Probably. But fortunately you're rich.

JOHN:  Well, yes, I am. But if I ................................................ all my money, what
................................................ ?

ROSE:  I'd say goodbye.

JOHN:  Now you're joking.

ROSE:  Oh no, I'm not!

**96** Read the article. For each number, write a comment beginning with **If**.

### Singing star Tanya announces wedding plans
– exclusive interview with Charlie Green

**CHARLIE:** Well, congratulations Tanya.

**TANYA:** Thank you. Of course, we're very excited about getting married, and frantically busy too, needless to say.

**CHARLIE:** I'm sure all your fans are longing to know how you met your fiance, Dr Radani.

**TANYA:** Well, it's a funny story really. (1) You know I did a world tour last year? That meant I had to spend five months travelling. (2) And I didn't have a holiday last year so I got terribly tired and stressed. (3) My manager panicked because he had contracted me to record a new album after the tour. (4) Anyway, the tour was such a huge success that I was able to postpone the recording for two months. I was really relieved. (5) My manager sent me to a luxury spa hotel for a complete rest. And I met this wonderful man, Hossein. He's a scientist. (6) He told me he should have been doing research in California, but he was recovering from a bad skiing accident. (7) We were the only guests on our own, so we started talking.

(8) He didn't know who I was. He didn't treat me like a star. He made me laugh. It was such a change. And that was it really. We found we'd fallen in love. (9) Wasn't it lucky my manager panicked? That's how I met my fiance!

**CHARLIE:** And what about your wedding plans?

**TANYA:** Ah, they're completely secret.

1 *If she hadn't done a world tour last year, she wouldn't have spent five months travelling.*

2

3

4

5

6

7

8

9

**97** What would you say in each situation? Begin each sentence with **If**.

1  *yesterday*          *today*

If I hadn't dyed my hair, my friends
wouldn't be laughing at me.

2  *yesterday*          *today*

TEST

If I hadn't revised thoroughly,
I wouldn't be able to do the test.

3  *yesterday*          *today*

4  *this morning*          *now*

I haven't got time
for breakfast!

I can't concentrate.

5  *last week*          *now*

I must remember to
phone and book seats.

BOOK NOW FOR CONCERT

BOOK NOW FOR SOLD OUT

6  *8 am*          *9.30 am*

Oh damn!

You're fired!

BUS

BOSS

7  *last weekend*          *today*

I'm sorry I won't
be at the wedding.

8  *this afternoon*          *now*

Do we need to
stop for petrol?

No, we've got more than
enough to get home.

1 MILE

# Conditionals: review

**98** Use your own ideas to complete the sentences.

1 What will you do if ___your plane is delayed___ ?

2 If he ___ he'd have more friends.

3 If I hadn't mended the TV, we ___ .

4 You wouldn't have felt ill if you ___ .

5 She ___ if she didn't gossip about her friends.

6 Will you forgive me if I ___ ?

7 If I ___ what would happen?

8 She would have won the competition if she ___ .

9 They wouldn't have minded if we ___ .

10 He ___ if he had listened to my advice.

**99** For each pair of sentences, complete sentence b so that it means the same as sentence a.

1 a You should go swimming regularly because that's a good way to get fit.
  b If you ___go swimming regularly, you'll get___ fit.

2 a Flying to Scotland is cheaper than going by rail. As a result, people go there by plane.
  b If flying ___weren't (wasn't) cheaper___ than going by rail, people ___wouldn't go___ there by plane.

3 a Cutting down rainforests has caused many plants and animals to disappear.
  b Many plants and animals ___wouldn't have disappeared___ if people ___hadn't cut down___ rainforests.

4 a I can't take a lot of exercise because I don't have enough free time.
  b If I ___ more free time, I ___ .

5 a Many students leave their bikes unlocked in the college yard. This makes life easy for thieves.
  b If students ___ in the college yard, life ___ .

6 a Some people didn't realise how dangerous smoking was when they were young. Now they are older they have serious health problems.
  b If people ___ when they were young, they ___ now they are older.

7 a Petra made some bread, but it didn't rise because she forgot to add yeast.
  b The bread ___ if Petra ___ .

8 a It's important to protect wildlife now. Otherwise there will be nothing left for future generations.
  b If we ___ , there ___ for future generations.

9 a Children don't realise how much toys cost, so they don't understand why they can't always have new ones.
  b If children ___ , they ___ why they can't always have new ones.

# I wish

**100**  Look at the pictures and write what each person wishes, using the words given.

1  be / tall and strong

    I wish I were tall and strong.

or    I wish I was tall and strong.

2  have / car

................................................................

3  work / office

................................................................

4  live / with my son

................................................................

5  can / swim

................................................................

6  not / live / city

................................................................

7  be / helicopter pilot

................................................................

8  not / have / short hair

................................................................

# I wish

**101**   Bernie and Martin share a room at college. Read what they say about each other.
Then write sentences beginning **I wish he would / wouldn't.**

MARTIN

It's dreadful having to share a room with Bernie. He borrows my phone without asking. He never washes his coffee mug and he's so untidy! He leaves his shoes lying around the room and drops his clothes on my chair – the room's such a mess I can't work. And he comes in late in the evening and doesn't remember I go to sleep early. Then he lies in bed playing computer games. I can't stand it! I'm going to look for a room on my own.

The trouble with Martin is that he never relaxes. He works so hard. He gets angry when I just make a phone call. And he interferes with my possessions. He moves my shoes and clothes around so I can't find them. He throws my shoes on my bed. He never plays computer games with me. He wakes me up when he goes out for a run early in the morning. He's no fun to share a room with.

BERNIE

Martin says:

I wish Bernie wouldn't borrow my phone without asking.

..................................................................................................................

..................................................................................................................

..................................................................................................................

..................................................................................................................

Bernie says:

I wish Martin would relax sometimes.

..................................................................................................................

..................................................................................................................

..................................................................................................................

..................................................................................................................

**102** Complete the conversations using **wish**.

**1** SUE: My mother's really angry with me.

PAM: Why?

SUE: Because she's found out where I was last weekend.

PAM: Oh, yes. I told her.

SUE: Well, I _wish you hadn't told_ (not / tell) her. It's not your business.

PAM: I'm sorry.

**2** TONY: Have you seen Ben's new jacket? I bet it was expensive.

ANA: He told me it cost him 700 Euros.

TONY: Wow! I .................................................. (have) as much money as him.

ANA: Well, you may not be rich, but you're much better looking than Ben.

TONY: Am I?

**3** GARY: You seem to enjoy dancing with Luke.

JANE: Yes, I do. He's a very good dancer.

GARY: I .................................................. (learn) to dance when I was young.

JANE: You could learn now.

GARY: Oh, I'd feel stupid in a dancing class at my age.

**4** EVA: I went to Indonesia last month.

MAY: Really? My brother's working in Jakarta now.

EVA: I .................................................. (realise). I could have met up with him.

MAY: Yes, it's a pity. You must tell me if you're going there again.

**5** FRED: My parents moved to São Paolo last month.

ALI: How do they like it?

FRED: My mother likes it, but my father misses the sea. He ..................................................
(not / move) there.

ALI: Perhaps he'll get used to it.

FRED: I doubt it.

**6** LUCY: You haven't seen my MP3 player, have you?

CHLOE: No, I haven't.

LUCY: I .................................................. (know) what I'd done with it.

CHLOE: I hope you didn't leave it in the taxi last night.

LUCY: So do I!

**7** KAY: My brothers are digging a swimming pool.

JILL: That sounds like hard work!

KAY: It is. Actually, I suspect they .................................................. (never / start). But
they can't stop now. There's a great big hole in the middle of the garden!

JILL: Yes, I see what you mean.

# The passive

**103** Complete the sentences using words from each box.

> build    design    develop    discover    discover
> invent    invent    ~~name~~    paint    play

> the Ancient Egyptians    Sir Tim Berners-Lee    the Chinese
> Crick and Watson    Marie Curie    Gustave Eiffel    ~~Eric the Red~~
> Johnny Depp    Guglielmo Marconi    Pablo Picasso

1 Greenland .....was named by Eric the Red................................. .
2 Captain Jack Sparrow ......................................................... .
3 The Pyramids .................................................................. .
4 The wireless .................................................................. .
5 Guernica ...................................................................... .
6 The World Wide Web ........................................................... .
7 The Statue of Liberty ......................................................... .
8 The structure of DNA .......................................................... .
9 Paper money .................................................................. .
10 Radium ....................................................................... .

**104** Put the verbs into the correct present perfect form, active or passive (**has done** or **has been done**).

① the woman / open
The woman has opened it.

② the fruit / eat
The fruit has been eaten.

③ the puncture / mend

④ the concert / cancel

⑤ Jane Jones / elect

⑥ the rabbit / disappear

⑦ the sculpture / steal

⑧ the students / pass

**105**   Rewrite this article using passive forms of the <u>underlined</u> verbs.

# DARING RAID AT LOCAL HOTEL

Thieves (1) <u>held</u> the manager of the Ridgeway Hotel at gunpoint last night during a daring raid in which they (2) <u>took</u> nearly £50,000 from the hotel safe. They also (3) <u>broke</u> into several of the bedrooms and (4) <u>removed</u> articles of value.

The thieves made their escape through the kitchen, where they (5) <u>damaged</u> several pieces of equipment. They (6) <u>injured</u> the chef when he tried to stop them and (7) <u>left</u> him lying unconscious on the floor. Police (8) <u>arrested</u> the thieves early this morning.

1   *The manager of the Ridgeway Hotel was held at gunpoint last night.*
2   ................................................................................................
3   ................................................................................................
4   ................................................................................................
5   ................................................................................................
6   ................................................................................................
7   ................................................................................................
8   ................................................................................................

**106**   Put the verbs into the correct passive form.

1   I've collected all the documents that ..... *are needed* ..... (need) for the house sale. Can you take them to the lawyer's office ..... *to be signed* ..... (sign)?

2   Look, this is a secret. Come into the garden where we ........................................... (not / overhear).

3   If you hadn't been so late for work, you ........................................... (not / sack).

4   This office is very inefficient. The phone ........................................... (never / answer) promptly, no proper records ........................................... (keep), and, worst of all, no reports ........................................... (written) since I started work here.

5   I was so worried about my garden while I was in hospital, but I have very good neighbours. When I got home, I could see that the vegetables ........................................... (water) every day and the grass ........................................... (cut) regularly.

6   Can you come to the police station? The man who ........................................... (suspect) of stealing your wallet ........................................... (arrest) and ........................................... (question) at the moment. The police hope he ........................................... (identify), either by you or another witness.

7   We had hoped to see several famous paintings, but the gallery ........................................... (reorganised) at the time of our visit and most of the really valuable works ........................................... (move) for safe keeping.

**107** There are mistakes in eight of these sentences. Correct the sentences where necessary. Write 'OK' if the sentence is already correct.

1 My neighbour is proud of her grandson <u>who born last week.</u>     who was born last week.

2 I'm very fond of this old brooch because it was belonged to my grandmother. ..........................................

3 My family live in Dubai, but I was educated in Switzerland. ..........................................

4 I'm afraid I can't lend you my car. It's repairing this week. ..........................................

5 The bridge was collapsed during the floods, but fortunately no-one was using it at the time. ..........................................

6 If you don't watch the barbecue carefully, someone will get burn. ..........................................

7 The word 'stupid' was in my report, but it wasn't referred to you. ..........................................

8 I'm sorry I'm late. I got held up in the traffic again. ..........................................

9 When did you realise that your bag had been disappeared? ..........................................

10 Children under the age of sixteen do not allow in the jacuzzi. ..........................................

**108** Choose the correct alternative.

Hi Sally,

How are you? I'm having a great time in Namibia. Our group is small and (1) ~~we were looked after~~ / <u>we're being looked after</u> very well by our guide. (2) <u>We've been shown</u> / <u>We were shown</u> some amazing things already and (3) <u>we've seen</u> / <u>we've been seen</u> some fantastic landscapes.

Last weekend we went to a National Park. (4) <u>We were driven</u> / <u>We were driving</u> to a watering hole where an amazing range of animals (5) <u>could be seeing</u> / <u>could be seen</u>. We were told that the numbers (6) <u>were risen</u> / <u>have risen</u> since the National Park (7) <u>founded</u> / <u>was founded</u>.

(8) <u>I'd been warned</u> / <u>I'd been warning</u> that the accommodation there was quite basic, but it was fine. (9) <u>We were given</u> / <u>We were giving</u> a big tent each, and there are outdoor showers and so on, which (10) <u>are kept</u> / <u>have kept</u> very clean.

Our guide tells us lots of funny stories. He (11) <u>was sent</u> / <u>sent</u> to South Africa by his family to work in a bank, but he (12) <u>hated</u> / <u>was hated</u> it. So he (13) <u>has behaved</u> / <u>behaved</u> very badly in order to (14) <u>get sacked</u> / <u>got sacked</u>. He kept us laughing for hours.

Tomorrow (15) <u>we'll be joined</u> / <u>we'll be joining</u> another group and going to see some rock paintings. (16) <u>They were discovered</u> / <u>They discovered</u> quite recently, so we're one of the first groups (17) <u>to be shown</u> / <u>to have shown</u> them.

I'll email again when I can (18) <u>get connected</u> / <u>have connected</u> to the Internet.

Love,

Maurice

**109** Complete the second sentence so that it has a similar meaning to the first sentence.
Do not use **by** unless it is important to the meaning.

**1** The instructor has marked all the assignments.
All the assignments _have been marked_ .

**2** My hairdresser kept me waiting for half an hour.
I _____ .

**3** The students must pay their own fees for this course.
The fees for this course _____ .

**4** Do you suppose your brother could have written that email?
Do you suppose that email _____ ?

**5** Solar panels supply all the power for this house.
All the power for this house _____ .

**6** During the summer, the cafe was employing more waiters every week.
During the summer, more waiters _____ .

**7** Nobody informed the police that there had been a mistake.
The police _____ .

**8** Where will your company send you next year?
Where will you _____ ?

**9** The news about the war worried Josephine.
Josephine _____ .

**10** I've still got the money because no-one has claimed it.
I've still got the money because it _____ .

**11** Has anyone ever asked you for your opinion?
Have you _____ ?

**12** People shouldn't allow children to watch that kind of TV programme.
Children _____ .

**13** All visitors must wear identity badges.
Identity badges _____ .

**14** Someone must have changed the time of the meeting.
The time of the meeting _____ .

**15** When will someone deliver the food for the party?
When _____ ?

**110** Put the verbs into the most suitable passive tense.

Alana has just met her boyfriend Grant in a coffee shop.

ALANA:   Hi! Sorry I'm late.

GRANT:   What kept you?

ALANA:   I came on the bus and (1) _it was stuck_ (it / stick) in a traffic jam for forty minutes.

GRANT:   Why didn't you just walk across the park as usual?

ALANA:   Because the park (2) ................................................ (close) since last weekend.

GRANT:   Why's that?

ALANA:   A celebrity tennis tournament (3) ................................................ (hold) there.

GRANT:   Do you know who (4) ................................................ (it / organise) by?

ALANA:   No, but I think the Williams sisters are competing in it. Someone told me
(5) ................................................ (they / see) at the Royal Hotel at the weekend.

GRANT:   Really?

ALANA:   Yeah. My friend said (6) ................................................ (they / fly) here in a
private plane by the organisers.

GRANT:   Well, if it's true, we're not going to the disco at the Royal this Friday.

ALANA:   Why not?

GRANT:   If they're there, the hotel (7) ................................................ (surround) by fans
and security guards.

ALANA:   But we might meet them if we go.

GRANT:   Don't be silly. They won't go to our local disco. And
(8) ................................................ (we / not invite) to their suite. In fact, the
disco (9) ................................................ (probably / cancel) if the hotel is full of
celebrities.

ALANA:   I suppose so. But we can go to the park gate now and see what's happening.
I heard that some local people
(10) ................................................

(recruit) yesterday, but I was too busy to go.
Perhaps

(11) ................................................

(we / employ) to sell programmes or
something.

GRANT:   OK, if you want to. But don't expect

(12) ................................................

(allow) anywhere near the big stars.

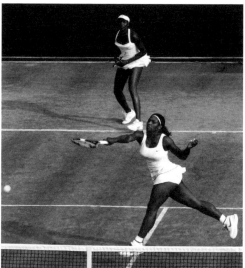

**111** Complete the sentences with the correct form of **get** where possible and a form of **be** in the others.

1 I never found that book we were looking for. It .....*got*..... lost when we moved house.

2 After the way he behaved last time he went to their house, it's unlikely he .............................. asked there again.

3 Naturally this vase is expensive. After all, it .............................. believed to be over three hundred years old.

4 I phoned to explain what had happened, but I .............................. cut off before I could finish.

5 There isn't any cheese left, I'm afraid. It .............................. eaten by the children.

6 He is a well-known expert on animal diseases and his opinions .............................. greatly respected.

7 My sister will be thrilled if her design .............................. chosen.

8 The book .............................. torn when the children started fighting over who should read it first.

9 Please don't touch anything on my desk. You .............................. supposed to answer the telephone, not tidy the office.

10 She was quite friendly at first, then she .............................. promoted and now she doesn't care about us any more.

**112** Complete the second sentence so that it has a similar meaning to the first sentence.

1 It is said that house prices are too high.
House prices .....*are said to be too high*......................................... .

2 It is thought that the hospital is short of money.
The hospital .............................................................................................. .

3 It was alleged that the athlete had cheated.
The athlete .............................................................................................. .

4 It is reported that the prime minister is resigning.
The prime minister ..................................................................................... .

5 It is expected that the new sports stadium will be finished soon.
The new sports stadium ............................................................................... .

6 It is generally considered that sixteen is too young to get married.
Sixteen ..................................................................................................... .

7 It was thought that the book had been destroyed.
The book ................................................................................................... .

8 It is believed that the children had been hiding for two weeks.
The children ............................................................................................... .

**113** Look at these notes made by a journalist. Then complete the article she wrote for her newspaper. Use verbs in the correct passive form.

Kitchen
6 am visit market, choose
        vegetables and fruit
7 am plan menu
8 am unload meat
9 am cook staff breakfast
9.30 am make desserts
10 am wash vegetables
clean fish
put meat in oven
mix salads

Dining-room
11 am vacuum floor
lay tables
arrange flowers
12pm open doors
serve about 200
        meals every lunchtime

**EATING OUT** with Eva Wolsey

It's exactly midday and I'm sitting in the Beverly Restaurant. Today I've been finding out just how much work goes on in a restaurant before the first customers arrive.

The staff have already done six hours work. The day began with a visit to the market where vegetables and fruit (1) ....were chosen.... . Back at the restaurant the menu (2) ............................ and then the day's delivery of meat (3) ............................ . After that, breakfast (4) ............................ for the staff. But they didn't have long to eat it, because by 9.30 it was time for the desserts (5) ............................ .

After the vegetables (6) ............................ , the fish (7) ............................ and the meat (8) ............................ in the oven.

While this was happening in the kitchen, in the dining-room the floor (9) ............................ . Since then, the tables (10) ............................ and the flowers (11) ............................ , so the dining-room looks fresh and pretty. In the last few minutes, salads (12) ............................ in the kitchen and in a moment the doors (13) ............................ . In the next three hours, about two hundred meals (14) ............................ !

# Have something done

**114** Tanya wants to rent a flat, but it needs some work before she can move in. She talks to the landlord and he agrees to her suggestions. Complete the conversation using **have** and the verbs in brackets.

TANYA:     This flat is in a good place, but there are a few problems.

LANDLORD:  Oh, really? What do you mean?

TANYA:     The mirror is broken.

LANDLORD:  (1) _I'll have it replaced._ (replace)

TANYA:     There are marks on the carpet.

LANDLORD:  (2) ........................................................................ (clean)

TANYA:     I don't like the colour of the walls.

LANDLORD:  (3) ........................................................................ (paint)

TANYA:     All the furniture is in the wrong rooms.

LANDLORD:  (4) ........................................................................ (rearrange)

TANYA:     One of the chairs is broken.

LANDLORD:  (5) ........................................................................ (mend)

TANYA:     Several of the cupboards are full of old clothes.

LANDLORD:  (6) ........................................................................ (empty)

TANYA:     The curtains are dirty.

LANDLORD:  (7) ........................................................................ (wash)

TANYA:     Then I might rent the flat.

**115** Rewrite the <u>underlined</u> words using **have something done**.

1 I didn't recognise Sheila because <u>the hairdresser's coloured her hair</u>.
   _She's had her hair coloured._

2 My laptop was very slow, so <u>a friend is going to install a new operating system for me</u>.

3 Gaby's parents <u>are going to ask a painter to paint her portrait</u>.

4 Simon has made a lot of money, so <u>an architect's designed him a fine new house</u>.

5 This room gets hot when the sun shines, so <u>I'm employing someone to fit blinds on the windows.</u>

6 I heard that Mrs Green didn't trust her husband, so <u>she hired a detective to follow him</u>!

7 My sister had always been self-conscious about her nose, so she has decided to go to a clinic <u>for an operation which will straighten it</u>.

# Questions

**116**    Wilma Shriek the pop singer has just arrived in London from America. She's being interviewed by a journalist. Look at the journalist's notes and Wilma's answers. Then write the journalist's questions.

1 how long / be here?            How long are you going to be here    ?    Two months.
2 be / first visit to this country?    Is this your first visit    ?    No, it isn't.
3 when / be here before?    _____    ?    Five years ago.
4 why / come then?    _____    ?    For a holiday.
5 why / come this time?    _____    ?    To work.
6 do / a tour now?    _____    ?    Yeah, that's right.
7 how many cities / visit?    _____    ?    About twenty.
8 what / want to do after that?    _____    ?    Have a holiday.
9 have / message for your fans?    _____    ?    Yeah – come to
                                                                        our concerts and
                                                                        have a wild time.

**117**    Lucy works in a tourist information office and has to answer a lot of questions. Read her answers and complete the questions using the words in brackets.

**1** TOURIST:  Do you know ____where the city maps are____ ? (city maps)
   LUCY:    Over there, on the other counter.

**2** TOURIST:  Can you tell me _____ ? (this guidebook)
   LUCY:    £9.99.

**3** TOURIST:  Please could you tell me _____ ? (postcards)
   LUCY:    They're on the third shelf, beside the window.

**4** TOURIST:  Do you happen to know _____ ? (the sports centre)
   LUCY:    Yes, it closes at half past ten on weekdays and ten at weekends.

**5** TOURIST:  Could you explain _____ ? (this timetable)
   LUCY:    It's quite simple. You find your destination on the left and read the times across the page.

**6** TOURIST:  I'd like to know _____ ? (free Internet access)
   LUCY:    It's available in most city centre coffee shops and the public library.

**7** TOURIST:  Do you know _____ ? (the music festival)
   LUCY:    The last weekend of July.

**8** TOURIST:  I can't remember _____ . (the castle)
   LUCY:    It was built about 1500, so that makes it over 500 years old.

**118** Sonia Schmidt is phoning to book a hotel room. Complete the conversation by putting the words in the correct order. Do not change the form of the words.

SONIA: Hello. My name's Sonia Schmidt. I'd like to book a room for myself and my husband please, starting from next Thursday.

RECEPTIONIST: Certainly. (1) staying / how many nights / you / be / will

How many nights will you be staying ?

SONIA: Three, probably.

RECEPTIONIST: Yes, we have a double room on those nights.

SONIA: (2) available / is / one with a sea view

............................................................................................................................................................ ?

RECEPTIONIST: Yes. By the way, (3) have / the special offer / about / are running / we / you / at the moment / heard

............................................................................................................................................................ ?

SONIA: Oh, no.

RECEPTIONIST: It's four nights for the price of three. (4) don't / take advantage / you / it / why / of

............................................................................................................................................................ ?

SONIA: (5) have / for it / what / I / to do / to qualify / got

............................................................................................................................................................ ?

RECEPTIONIST: Just make a definite booking today and let me have your credit card number. We won't use it until you leave.

SONIA: OK. (6) be / much / will / it / how / for bed and breakfast

............................................................................................................................................................ ?

RECEPTIONIST: For three nights, £60 per person per night, plus the fourth night and breakfast free. So that's £360 all together.

SONIA: Yes. I think I'll do that. We can stay till Monday. (7) you / give / my credit card number / I / shall / now

............................................................................................................................................................ ?

RECEPTIONIST: Yes please.

SONIA: 3434 8123 7650 9920.

RECEPTIONIST: Thank you very much. (8) would / to / me / you / email / like / confirmation of your reservation / you / to

............................................................................................................................................................ ?

SONIA: Yes, please. To soniaschmidt@numail.com.

RECEPTIONIST: Thank you. We'll look forward to seeing you.

SONIA: Thank you, goodbye.

**119** Brian's doctor has advised him to join a Health Club. The instructor is going to help him to plan his fitness programme. Write the instructor's questions. Read the whole conversation before you begin.

INSTRUCTOR: OK, Brian. Let's find out how fit you are. (1) First of all, <u>how old are you</u> ?

BRIAN: I'm thirty-two.

INSTRUCTOR: (2) And .......................................................... ?

BRIAN: About seventy-five kilos.

INSTRUCTOR: (3) And .......................................................... ?

BRIAN: One metre eighty.

INSTRUCTOR: (4) .......................................................... ?

BRIAN: I work in a call centre for a bank.

INSTRUCTOR: Really? (5) So, .......................................................... ?

BRIAN: Well, I take some exercise, but it's not regular.

INSTRUCTOR: (6) .......................................................... ?

BRIAN: No, I haven't done any sport since I left school. I sometimes go for a walk on my day off if the weather's good.

INSTRUCTOR: I see. (7) .......................................................... ?

BRIAN: Yes, I admit I do. Not more than a packet a day, though.

INSTRUCTOR: That's quite a lot, actually. (8) .......................................................... ?

BRIAN: Well, I tried once, about a year ago, but then I started putting on weight. But my doctor says I must try again.

INSTRUCTOR: Well, we can give you some help with that too. It's really important, you know. Now if you'll come with me, I'm going to do a few checks and then we'll make a plan for you.

BRIAN: OK. Thanks.

**120** There are mistakes in eight of these sentences. Correct the sentences where necessary. Write 'OK' if the sentence is already correct.

1 Have ever you been to Hawaii?          <u>Have you ever been</u>

2 What is this word mean?          ..........................................

3 How much costs it to fly to Australia from here?          ..........................................

4 We can't remember where did we leave our car.          ..........................................

5 Had the film started when you turned the TV on?          ..........................................

6 Would you like to explain what is your problem?          ..........................................

7 How long did it you take to get here?          ..........................................

8 Now I know why didn't you tell me what were you buying!          ..........................................

9 Can you tell me where the dictionaries are kept?          ..........................................

10 Why young people don't show more respect to the elderly?          ..........................................

# Reported speech and questions

**121** Read the email. Then write what Angela actually said to Della.

**From:** Della Rigby
**To:** Maggie Clark
**Subject:** Angela

Hi Maggie,

Guess what? Last week I met Angela, who we used to work with. She told me she was still living with her parents, but she wanted to move out. She explained that her sister had found a flat they could share, and they'd looked round it the week before. It had just been decorated and they'd liked it very much, but they'd been asked to pay a month's rent in advance. Unfortunately, because she was working part-time and she didn't earn much money, she hadn't saved enough for the deposit. She said she was going to get a new job. She was being interviewed the next day, so she had to buy some new clothes for the interview. I hope Angela and her sister will invite us to their new flat when they move in!

Love,
Della

*ANGELA*

I'm still living with my parents, but

**122** In Exercise 41, Alex, who wanted to go to an art college, was interviewed by one of the lecturers. A year later, his friend Charlie asked him about the interview, as he wanted to go to the same college. Complete Alex's answers.

CHARLIE: So, Alex, what was the interview like?

ALEX: Well, the interviewer started by asking me when I (1) ....I'd left.... (leave) school. And then he wanted to know where I (2) ................................. (be) since then. I told him I (3) ................................. (have) several jobs. First I (4) ................................. (work) in a cafe for about a year because I (5) ................................. (need) to save a lot of money for travelling. Of course he asked me where I (6) ................................. (want) to go and when I told him, he asked whether I (7) ................................. (visit) all those places. I explained to him that I (8) ................................. (be) to Brazil and Peru, and I (9) ................................. (spend) some months in Turkey. He told me I (10) ................................. (be) very lucky. Then he asked if I (11) ................................. (bring) some work to show him and he looked at my work. He liked it, I think.

CHARLIE: Was that all?

ALEX: I think so. He asked me when I (12) ................................. (become) interested in painting and drawing, and I said that I (13) ................................. (think) I always (14) ................................. (be). Oh, yes, and he told me my work (15) ................................. (be) very good.

CHARLIE: I'm not surprised. It is good. I hope he'll like my stuff too.

ALEX: Oh, I think he will, actually.

**123** Look back at your answers to Exercise 116. Complete the article which the journalist wrote a month after the interview with Wilma.

Last month I was lucky enough to interview Wilma Shriek when she was in this country. I asked her how long she (1) ....was going to be.... here and she said two months, but actually she has already gone back to America. She told me it (2) ................................. her first visit because she (3) ................................. here five years before, for a holiday. She told me she (4) ................................. a tour. When I asked her how many cities she (5) ................................. , she thought about twenty. She said she (6) ................................. to have a holiday after the tour. She looked tired. But when I asked her whether she (7) ................................. a message for her fans, she told them (8) ................................. to the concerts and have a wild time. Well, it looks as though Wilma has had too many wild times, because her manager said last week that she is now resting!

**124** John had a row with his girlfriend, Julie. His friend Mark tried to help them get back together and talked to Julie for John.

MARK: Julie, John's asked me to talk to you.

JULIE: I don't want to speak to him.

MARK: Look Julie, John's really upset.

JULIE: I'm upset too.

MARK: Will you just let me tell you his side of the story?

JULIE: I'm not interested. He promised to meet me at the restaurant, but he didn't turn up. I don't want to see him again.

MARK: But Julie, his car had broken down.

JULIE: So? I had my phone with me.

MARK: But that's the point. He tried to phone, but he couldn't get through.

JULIE: I don't believe he tried.

MARK: Yes, he did. His phone wasn't working, so he came to my flat and tried on my landline. Do you believe me?

JULIE: OK, I'll talk to him. Listen, I'm going to be late for work. I'll meet him at six o'clock in the square.

MARK: Thanks, Julie. He'll be really happy. And I promise he'll be there.

**Complete the conversation Mark had later with John.**

JOHN: What did Julie say?

MARK: She said she (1) _didn't want to speak to you_ .

JOHN: Well, what did she say when you told her I was really upset?

MARK: She said she (2) .......................................................... too, so I asked her to let me explain your side of the story. She said she (3) .......................................................... . You (4) .......................................................... to meet her at the restaurant, but you (5) .......................................................... . She said she (6) .......................................................... again.

JOHN: Did you explain about the car?

MARK: Yes, and she said she (7) .......................................................... her phone with her. So I explained you couldn't get through, but she said she (8) .......................................................... you (9) .......................................................... . Then I told her you (10) .......................................................... to my flat and (11) .......................................................... on my landline. I asked her (12) .......................................................... me. I think she did. Anyway, she said she (13) .......................................................... to you. Then she said she (14) .......................................................... late for work, so we had to finish. You have to meet her in the square at six o'clock.

JOHN: Thanks, Mark. I really appreciate what you've done for me.

MARK: That's OK. Just don't be late this evening.

**125** You've just arrived at the Great Bay Hotel for a holiday. It's not the same as your travel agent told you it would be. Look at your travel agent's website and complete the email you send to the travel agent.

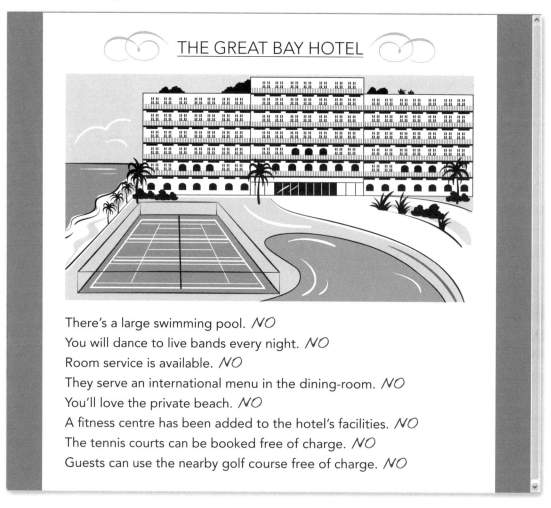

THE GREAT BAY HOTEL

There's a large swimming pool. *NO*
You will dance to live bands every night. *NO*
Room service is available. *NO*
They serve an international menu in the dining-room. *NO*
You'll love the private beach. *NO*
A fitness centre has been added to the hotel's facilities. *NO*
The tennis courts can be booked free of charge. *NO*
Guests can use the nearby golf course free of charge. *NO*

**To:** Mr Smiley, Sunways Travel Agency

I am very disappointed because the Great Bay Hotel is quite different from what
you told us. You said there ....*was a large swimming pool*.... and that we

.................................................................................................

You also said ...........................................................................

The website said ......................................................................

You told us ................................................................................

In fact, none of these facilities is available. Please arrange for us to be transferred to a better
hotel immediately.

**126**

Anna has just met the singer Colin Boyle. (You may remember him from Exercise 16.) She is telling Ian, about the meeting. Ian wants to know exactly what Colin said to Anna and what she said to him.

IAN:    Well, what was he like? Was he friendly? What did he say?

ANNA:    He was really friendly. (1) <u>He asked me who I was</u>.

IAN:    Then what?

ANNA:    (2) <u>He asked me where I came from</u>.

IAN:    And what did you say?

ANNA:    (3) <u>I told him I came from Dublin</u>, of course. Then (4) <u>he said that was where he was born too</u>. Then (5) <u>I told him I'd been a fan of his for ages</u> and (6) <u>he said that was very good to hear</u>. Then (7) <u>he asked whether I was going to the concert tonight</u>. So (8) <u>I told him we wanted to, but we hadn't been able to get tickets</u>. (9) <u>He asked if the tickets were sold out</u>, and (10) <u>I told him they'd sold all but the most expensive ones and we couldn't afford those</u>.

IAN:    And did he give you some tickets?

ANNA:    No, he didn't. But (11) <u>he asked the concert hall manager if we could have some at the cheaper price</u>. And the manager said 'Yes'!

Now write exactly what Anna and Colin said.

**1** Colin asked: ___Who are you?___

**2** Colin asked: ...........................................................................................................

**3** Anna said: ...........................................................................................................

**4** Colin said: ...........................................................................................................

**5** Anna said: ...........................................................................................................

**6** Colin said: ...........................................................................................................

**7** Colin asked: ...........................................................................................................

**8** Anna said: ...........................................................................................................

**9** Colin asked: ...........................................................................................................

**10** Anna said: ...........................................................................................................

**11** Colin asked the concert hall manager: ...................................................................

**127**

Imagine that when you were on holiday last year you met someone famous. This could be a musician, a film star, a sportsman or woman, a politician, etc. Look at what Anna told Ian in Exercise 126 and write an email to a friend about the conversation you had.

**From:**
**To:**
**Subject:**

Hi!

I never told you that when I was on holiday last year I met .......................................

.........................................................................................................................

.........................................................................................................................

.........................................................................................................................

.........................................................................................................................

.........................................................................................................................

.........................................................................................................................

**128** Rewrite the sentences beginning in the way shown.

1 'Where are you going?' asked Tom.
  *Tom asked (me) where I was going* .

2 'Where are you going to spend the holiday?' asked Mike.
  Mike asked ........................................................................................................................................ .

3 'What will you do when you leave school?' asked Jennifer.
  Jennifer asked .................................................................................................................................... .

4 'How did you know my name?' the journalist asked the security guard.
  The journalist wanted to know ........................................................................................................... .

5 'Do you have an appointment?' asked the clerk.
  The clerk asked .................................................................................................................................. .

6 'Have you seen the blue memory stick?' Bernard asked his wife.
  Bernard wondered .............................................................................................................................. .

7 'Why didn't Isobel phone me?' asked her brother.
  Isobel's brother wanted to know ........................................................................................................ .

8 'Will you carry my laptop for me please, Rosemary?' Richard asked.
  Richard asked ..................................................................................................................................... .

9 'When can I see the doctor?' Charles asked the receptionist.
  Charles asked ..................................................................................................................................... .

**129** Complete the sentences with the correct form of **say** or **tell**.

1 *Did you tell* (you) your brother the truth about that money?

2 What ............................................ (you) to Wendy last night? She looks terribly upset this morning.

3 Is something wrong? Can you ............................................ me about it?

4 My English teacher keeps asking me ............................................ the class a joke from my
  country, but I can't think of any suitable ones!

5 If I asked you to marry me, what ............................................ (you)?

6 I never know what ............................................ to people when they pay me a compliment.

7 Don't worry, I'm sure the boys are fine. Anyway, I ............................................ them to call me if
  they had any problems.

8 I'll never speak to him again after all the lies he ............................................ me last weekend.

9 If I were you, I ............................................ (not) anything about your problems now.

10 Promise you ............................................ (not) anything to my girlfriend. She'll be furious if she
  finds out what I've done.

11 I ............................................ (already) you, I don't know where your phone is.

12 Please ............................................ you'll forgive me. I'm really sorry for all the trouble I've
  caused.

13 I'm ready to serve the meal. Can you ............................................ the children to go and wash
  their hands, please?

**130** Complete the email with the correct form of **say** or **tell**.

> **From:** Neville Cripps
> **To:** Stephanie Peters
> **Subject:** Talk with my dad
>
> Hello Stephanie,
>
> I must (1) ....*tell*.... you about the talk I had with my dad last weekend.
> We talked for hours and I (2) ................................................................. him all about
> the plans we've made for our business. At first, he wasn't very interested, he
> (3) ................................................................. he didn't think we were old enough to run a
> business. But then I (4) ................................................................. him that we had already
> talked to a small business adviser, and she (5) .................................................................
> that the plan seemed realistic. She agreed that all we need is a small loan at a
> reasonable rate.
>
> So after that he sat down and asked me (6) ................................................................. him
> exactly how much money we'd need to start with, and how long for. Eventually he
> (7) ................................................................. to me, 'OK, it's a good plan.
> (8) ................................................................. Stephanie that I'll lend you the money to get
> started.' Honestly, I couldn't believe he (9) ................................................................. it!
> Isn't it great? I'm really looking forward to seeing you next week so we can talk to him
> together and get things going.
>
> All the best,
> Neville

**131** There are mistakes in four of these sentences. Correct the sentences where necessary.
Write 'OK' if the sentence is already correct.

1 Joan <u>said she had been very happy</u> in her new job          <u>said she was very happy</u>
   and liked her new boss better than her old one.          .............................................

2 Michael explained that he couldn't come to the party          .............................................
   because he was working that evening.

3 We had a great evening with Janet. She was saying          .............................................
   us about her fascinating trip to Kenya.

4 I'm sorry to bother you, but you said to call if I was worried.    .............................................

5 We were disappointed when the receptionist told that          .............................................
   the hotel was fully booked that week.

6 The museum guard asked the visitors to not touch the exhibits.   .............................................

7 The tour guide explained that the Severn is the          .............................................
   longest river in England.

# –ing and infinitive

**132** Put the verbs into the correct form: **–ing** or infinitive.

1  I don't get on with the new boss, so I've asked ....to be transferred.... (transfer) to another branch of the company.

2  Please stop ....interrupting.... (interrupt) me when I'm explaining something to you. You can ask questions at the end.

3  He admits ........................ (enter) the house, but he says he didn't take anything.

4  What a dreadful man! Can you imagine ........................ (live) with him?

5  I've forgotten ........................ (bring) my briefcase with me. I'll have to go back for it.

6  We had hoped ........................ (live) in our new house by now, but the builders are still working on it.

7  I don't mind ........................ (work) late if it will help at all.

8  You'll just have to find a job. I simply can't afford ........................ (support) you any longer.

**133** Put the verbs into the correct form: **–ing** or infinitive.

> # CYCLIST ABANDONS 24 HR RIDE
>
> For the second time, Andrew Spicer, the local cycling star, has decided (1) _to give up_
> (give up) the attempt (2) ............................................ (ride) his bike non-stop for twenty-four
> hours. His decision came after poor weather conditions had caused him to postpone
> (3) ............................................ (set off) for several hours. His first attempt had also ended in
> failure, when he appeared (4) ............................................ (lose) control of his bicycle as he
> attempted to avoid (5) ............................................ (hit) a
> small child and crashed into a wall. He says that he has not yet
> decided whether (6) ............................................ (try)
> one more time, but denies (7) ............................................
> (lose) interest in the project. 'I've promised
> (8) ............................................ (raise) money for the local
> hospital,' he explained. 'They deserve help. I shall do what
> I can if I manage (9) ............................................ (find)
> the time.'

**134** Complete the conversations with suitable verbs in the correct form: **–ing** or infinitive.

**A** ANN: What are you doing this weekend?

   BILL: I'm hoping (1) _to visit_ my brother at his university if I can.

   ANN: I thought you went to see him last weekend.

   BILL: No, I was planning (2) ............................................ him then, but he emailed
me and suggested (3) ............................................ the visit for a week
because he hadn't finished (4) ............................................ his thesis.
Now he's done it, we can celebrate.

**B** CILLA: Can you help me get these packages posted today? One of our main customers has said
he'll consider (5) ............................................ to another supplier if we don't
improve our delivery times.

   DAVE: Have we been failing (6) ............................................ on time? I didn't know that.

   CILLA: Apparently someone forgot (7) ............................................ one order last
month. So I agreed (8) ............................................ them myself this time –
we can't risk (9) ............................................ such an important customer.

**C** JACK: Oh dear, here's another email from Peter.

   SEAN: Why does he keep (10) ............................................ you?

   JACK: He wants me to join his basketball team. He's offered (11) ............................................
me fix my car if I agree (12) ............................................ them. The trouble is, I'd
have to go to a lot of training sessions and I haven't got time. And I can fix the car by myself.

   SEAN: Well, you'll just have to find a way to say no. You can't avoid
(13) ............................................ to him forever.

**135** Complete the sentences using **–ing** or infinitive.

1   TERRY   Can you help me?   CHRIS

    Terry wanted Chris _to help him_ .

2   You're late again! Do fifty press-ups!   COACH   HUGO

    The coach ordered ...........................................

3   CASHIER

    The gangsters forced ...........................................

4   DELLA   LAURA   I wish I'd never bought those drums.

    Laura regretted ...........................................

5   FELICITY   You're not going out until you've finished your homework.   CHARLIE

    Felicity made ...........................................

6   Shampoo   soap   JOHN

    John tried ...........................................

7   The car needed ...........................................

8   SANDY   JIM

    Jim helped ...........................................

**136** Complete the conversations with the correct form of the verbs and any other words you need.

**A** PAT: Who should I ask if I want a day off?

MICK: It doesn't really matter, except I'd advise (1) ___you not to ask___ (not / ask) the assistant manager. He can be very rude sometimes.

PAT: Oh, I don't mind (2) ................................................. (shout) at by him. He threatened (3) ................................................. (sack) me last week, but he apologised very politely later.

**B** SUE: I don't trust the new director of marketing.

JILL: Why not?

SUE: Well, she claims (4) ................................................. (work) in several different countries before she came here. But when I asked her where exactly, she kept (5) ................................................. (change) the subject. I was wondering whether (6) ................................................. (say) something to the boss.

JILL: Perhaps she's just shy. Why don't we go on (7) ................................................. (be) friendly for a few more days and see how she behaves?

SUE: OK. I'd hate (8) ................................................. (get) someone into trouble for nothing.

**C** ANDY: I don't know what to do about Gemma. She's so difficult to work with. She keeps forgetting (9) ................................................. (pass) on important messages and she won't let me (10) ................................................. (help) her when she's busy.

JOAN: Have you actually talked to her about all this?

ANDY: That's part of the problem. I've tried (11) ................................................. (discuss) the problem with her, but she always says she's too busy to stop and talk. I've even tried (12) ................................................. (ask) her to have lunch with me, but she doesn't want to.

JOAN: I think I'd better have a chat with her. How long has she been like this?

ANDY: Oh, it's several weeks now.

JOAN: Well, I'd really like (13) ................................................. (know) about the problem earlier. Never mind, I'll see what I can do.

ANDY: Thanks very much.

**137** Complete the sentences with your own ideas. Use **–ing** or the infinitive.

**1** I often help ___to prepare lunch at weekends___ .

**2** I learnt ................................................. at the age of .................... .

**3** I can't help ................................................. when I see someone being treated unfairly.

**4** I don't mind ................................................. , but I hate ................................................. .

**5** I sometimes pretend ................................................. when really I'm just daydreaming.

**6** I always encourage ................................................. which I have enjoyed reading myself.

**7** I remember ................................................. when I was a small child.

**8** I enjoy ................................................. even though I'm not very good at it.

**9** I expect ................................................. by the end of next year.

**10** I've given up ................................................. .

# Prepositions and expressions + –ing

## 138

Match the beginning of each sentence with the most suitable ending.

**How to study efficiently**

| | | |
|---|---|---|
| 1 Begin by | a making plans you can't possibly keep. | 1 ___b___ |
| 2 Be realistic: there's no point in | b ~~making a list of what you have to do.~~ | 2 _____ |
| 3 Find a quiet place where you can work without | c studying. | 3 _____ |
| 4 If possible, use this place only for | d marking each topic on your list as you complete it. | 4 _____ |
| 5 Check you have everything you need before | e jumping up to fetch things every five minutes. | 5 _____ 6 _____ |
| 6 This means you won't waste time | f being interrupted. | 7 _____ |
| 7 Encourage yourself by | g starting work. | |

## 139

Use the notes to complete the advice below. Use –ing and a preposition if necessary.

1 Read through the exam paper carefully.
2 Check the instructions.
3 Don't spend too long on one question.
4 Don't try to see how your friends are getting on.
5 Allow time to check all your answers.
6 Cheats rarely do well in the long run.

**How to take exams**

1 Begin __by reading through the exam paper carefully__ .
2 Make sure you know exactly what to do _____ .
3 There's no point _____ .
4 Don't waste time _____ .
5 Avoid careless mistakes _____ .
6 It's rarely worth _____ .

## 140

Complete the pieces of advice. Use –ing and your own ideas.

1 It's rude to borrow people's things without __asking their permission first__ .
2 You should eat a healthy diet instead of _____ .
3 You won't get rich by _____ .
4 You must always thank people for _____ .
5 You shouldn't insist on _____ .
6 It's dangerous to go walking in the mountains without _____ .
7 It's good manners to apologise for _____ .
8 You should check delivery charges before _____ .

# I'm used to doing and I used to do

**141** Put the verbs into the correct form.

Dear Ruth,

Thanks very much for the lovely present you sent for Laurie. It was very kind of you. You say in your note that you haven't got used to (1) _being_ (be) an aunt yet. I used to (2) _think_ (think) that becoming a father wouldn't change me. I was wrong, of course! Life will never be the same again. We never used to (3) ........................................ (go) to bed before midnight, but now we're asleep by ten because we've had to get used to (4) ........................................ (wake) up at five o'clock. Actually, in a way, that's good. I always used to (5) ........................................ (arrive) late at the office, but since Laurie was born my colleagues have got used to (6) ........................................ (find) me hard at work by the time they arrive!

I should say, though, it hasn't been so easy for Jenny. At first she found it very hard on her own with Laurie. She wasn't used to (7) ........................................ (spend) all day alone with a baby. But now she's got to know a neighbour who also has a young baby and that helps. She used to (8) ........................................ (say) she'd go back to work when Laurie was six months, but now she's used to (9) ........................................ (be) at home she's beginning to enjoy herself, so she may wait until Laurie is a bit older.

Anyway, try to come and see us soon while Laurie is still small.

All the best,
Dennis

# To ... and preposition + –ing
(**Afraid to do** and **afraid of doing**)

**142** Complete the conversations. Use a preposition + –ing or the infinitive.

**A** Sid and Tom are walking through the town centre.

SID: Look, there's Angela. Isn't she stunning?

TOM: She's all right. You really fancy her, don't you?

SID: Yeah. I often dream (1) *about taking* (take) her out, but I'm afraid (2) *to ask* (ask) her.

TOM: Why?

SID: Well, I suppose I'm afraid (3) .................................................. (look) like a fool if she refuses.

TOM: If you like her so much, you shouldn't be afraid (4) .................................................. (risk) it. Anyway, I'm sure she won't refuse.

SID: You think so?

TOM: Yeah, go on, why don't you text her?

SID: OK, I'll do it now.

TOM: It's lucky for me that I've succeeded (5) .................................................. (persuade) you.

SID: Why's that?

TOM: I just happen to know she fancies you. I told her I'd get you to contact her and she's looking forward (6) .................................................. (hear) from you!

**B** Brian and Phil are at work.

BRIAN: Good morning Phil, could we have a word in my office?

PHIL: Of course.

BRIAN: I'm sorry (7) .................................................. (have) to say this, but I'm afraid you failed (8) .................................................. (achieve) high enough sales to earn a bonus this month. I suppose the bad weather kept the customers away?

PHIL: Yes, I guess so. I'm very sorry (9) .................................................. (let) you down this time.

BRIAN: OK, I'm sure you'll make it up soon. I'm thinking (10) .................................................. (send) one or two junior sales staff on a course next month. Would you be interested (11) .................................................. (go)?

PHIL: Yes, I would be. Thank you.

BRIAN: Good. I'll put your name on the list.

**C** Joanna has phoned Katie.

JOANNA: I'm sorry (12) .................................................. (forget) your birthday last week.

KATIE: That's OK. You were in the middle of your exams. You're allowed (13) .................................................. (forget) people's birthdays on exam days!

JOANNA: That shouldn't have prevented me (14) .................................................. (send) you a card. Did you get some from the family?

KATIE: Well, Mum was the only one (15) .................................................. (remember).

JOANNA: Well, she's not likely (16) .................................................. (forget), is she?

KATIE: No, I suppose you're right.

# Verb forms: review

**143** Put the verbs in the correct form. Can you solve this detective puzzle?

Trevor Stern was not a popular man, in spite of his wealth.
He (1) ...*lived*... (live) in a large house about a mile outside
the village of Prenton. When he (2) ...*was found*... (find)
dead in his study, no-one (3) ...*cried*... (cry),
not even his only daughter. It was soon clear that he
(4) ................................................ (murder).

Detective Inspector Blackledge took statements from
his widow Delia, his fifteen-year-old daughter Lucy,
his business partner Gerald Brook, and his doctor.

Delia gave her statement first.

*DELIA*

I (5) ................................................ (not / love) my husband, he was a cold and
selfish man. But I (6) ................................................ (not / murder) him, either.
After dinner last night he said he (7) ................................................ (want) to
check some business papers in his study. He (8) ................................................
(have) a meeting with Gerald, his business partner, the next morning.
He (9) ................................................ (ask) for some tea. That was about nine
o'clock. I (10) ................................................ (watch) a rather exciting film, so I
(11) ................................................ (tell) Lucy to take it to him.

At quarter past nine Doctor Emerson (12) ................................................ (call).
I (13) ................................................ (notice) the time because we (14) ................................................
(expect) him to come earlier. I (15) ................................................ (answer) the front door bell. Trevor
(16) ................................................ (shout) in his study. He and Lucy (17) ................................................
(obviously / have) a serious row. So I (18) ................................................ (take) the doctor into the
sitting-room for a moment. Then Trevor stopped (19) ................................................ (shout). I guessed
Lucy (20) ................................................ (go) out by the back door. Doctor Emerson went to the
study. I think he wanted to persuade Trevor (21) ................................................ (go) into hospital for
some tests, but Trevor (22) ................................................ (not / want) to go.

I (23) ................................................ (hear) my husband shouting again several times over the next
twenty minutes. He called Emerson an ignorant country doctor and later he said something like,
'There's nothing you can do!' I think Lucy (24) ................................................ (come) back into the
house while the doctor (25) ................................................ (still / talk) to Trevor.
I (26) ................................................ (hear) the front door bang during a moment of quiet when Trevor
(27) ................................................ (not / shout). I was tired and fed up, and went to my bedroom
soon after that. My sister (28) ................................................ (phone) and we
(29) ................................................ (talk) for ages. I (30) ................................................ (tell) her I
(31) ................................................ (decide) to leave Trevor.

LUCY

Mum (32) ............................................ (watch) a stupid film after dinner, so she made me (33) ............................................ (take) Dad's tea into his study. It was about nine o'clock. He was in a really mean mood. He shouted at me because I (34) ............................................ (spill) a few drops of tea on his desk while I (35) ............................................ (pour) it. I (36) ............................................ (not / want) to watch the film with Mum, so I (37) ............................................ (creep) out of the house by the back door. I (38) ............................................ (decide) to go down to the village and text my boyfriend Alan to meet me outside his house. I (39) ............................................ (never / tell) Mum or Dad when I (40) ............................................ (see) him. Especially yesterday, because Dad and I (41) ............................................ (have) a stupid argument about Alan the day before.

It (42) ............................................ (usually / take) quarter of an hour to walk to the village. Perhaps it (43) ............................................ (take) less time last night. I can't prove I (44) ............................................ (go) to the village. No-one (45) ............................................ (see) me while I (46) ............................................ (walk) there. I (47) ............................................ (see) Gerald, that's Dad's business partner. He (48) ............................................ (stand) near the window in his sitting-room. He (49) ............................................ (not / see) me though, because it was dark outside. He (50) ............................................ (talk) on the phone, I think. Alan (51) ............................................ (not / answer) my text by the time I (52) ............................................ (reach) his house. Then I (53) ............................................ (remember) he (54) ............................................ (play) in a concert that evening. So I (55) ............................................ (walk) home again. I (56) ............................................ (meet) Gerald just before I (57) ............................................ (reach) our house. He (58) ............................................ (look) for his dog. That was about twenty to ten. I came in by the back door as quietly as possible and went to bed. I didn't want to see my parents again that evening.

DOCTOR EMERSON

I (59) ............................................ (call) at the Sterns' house at 9.15. I (60) ............................................ (be) rather later than I (61) ............................................ (plan) to be because I (62) ............................................ (visit) another patient. When Mrs Stern (63) ............................................ (let) me into the house, she (64) ............................................ (seem) rather embarrassed and (65) ............................................ (show) me into the sitting-room. I could hear Trevor Stern (66) ............................................ (shout) at someone in his study. Mrs Stern said something about teenage girls and that they (67) ............................................ (have) problems with Lucy. Well, the shouting (68) ............................................ (stop) almost immediately, so I (69) ............................................ (go) to his study. Lucy (70) ............................................ (already / leave) the room before I (71) ............................................ (get) there. I tried (72) ............................................ (explain) to Trevor why he needed (73) ............................................ (have) these hospital tests, but he (74) ............................................ (not / listen). He said I (75) ............................................ (be) an ignorant country doctor who (76) ............................................ (not / know) what he (77) ............................................ (talk) about. I (78) ............................................ (realise) it was no use (79) ............................................ (argue) with him, so I (80) ............................................ (leave) after only a few minutes. I was quite angry actually. I let myself out of the house without (81) ............................................ (see) Lucy or Mrs Stern.

# Verb forms: review

Yes, Trevor was my business partner. We (82) ................................ (not / be) really friends. Yes, my house (83) ................................ (be) just round the corner from the Sterns'. I (84) ................................ (live) here for two years now. I (85) ................................ (have) a little cottage in the village. But I (86) ................................ (buy) this house when I started (87) ................................ (earn) a lot of money.

I can't really tell you very much about the night Trevor died. I took my dog for a long walk that evening. I (88) ................................ (go) up on the hills, away from the village. Then the stupid dog (89) ................................ (run) after a rabbit or something and I (90) ................................ (lose) him in the dark. I (91) ................................ (look) for him when I (92) ................................ (meet) Lucy, as a matter of fact. She (93) ................................ (walk) up the road towards their house. She (94) ................................ (seem) rather upset. I told her I (95) ................................ (look) for my dog, but she said she (96) ................................ (not / see) it.

She (97) ................................ (go) into her house and I (98) ................................ (find) the dog a few minutes afterwards. I was back home by just after quarter to ten.

GERALD

Detective Inspector Blackledge showed the statements to her colleague, Sergeant Ross.

BLACKLEDGE: Well, Ross. What do you think? Who killed Stern?

ROSS: I don't know. It (99) ................................ (not / be) his wife. She (100) ................................ (not / even / go) into the study.

BLACKLEDGE: But she admits she didn't love him. Do you think she's in love with the doctor?

ROSS: It's possible. And perhaps Trevor Stern (101) ................................ (find out). But we know the doctor was at the hospital by ten o'clock that night. And that's at least half an hour from the Sterns' house.

BLACKLEDGE: But that (102) ................................ (mean) he (103) ................................ (leave) the Sterns' house before half past nine.

ROSS: Exactly. Also, Delia Stern told her sister she (104) ................................ (leave) her husband. She didn't need (105) ................................ (murder) him.

BLACKLEDGE: Yes, and there's something about Lucy's story which doesn't quite fit. Let's see, what did Gerald Brook say?

ROSS: That's it! Lucy (106) ................................ (not / walk) to the village and back if he (107) ................................ (meet) her at twenty to ten. She (108) ................................ (still / shout at) by her father at 9.15.

BLACKLEDGE: But look at all the statements. The times don't fit.

ROSS: Neither do the facts. Someone (109) ................................ (tell) lies.

BLACKLEDGE: I think it's time we (110) ................................ (make) an arrest.

Who did they arrest? See page 120.

# Countable and uncountable

**144** Some of these sentences need **a/an**. Correct the sentences where necessary.

1 Joanna eats apple every morning.     *an apple*
2 Peter doesn't like milk in his tea.     *OK*
3 Katie rarely has biscuit with her coffee.
4 George normally eats meat for dinner.
5 Brian usually has omelette for lunch.
6 Margaret never drinks beer.

**145** Lizzie is training to run in a marathon. Every day she writes down how far she runs and what she eats. Look at the pictures of what she ate today and complete what she wrote, using **a/an** where necessary.

BREAKFAST    LUNCH    DINNER

## Monday
I ran 15 km. I had (1) *cereal* and (2) ........................... for
breakfast. At lunchtime I ate (3) ........................... and
(4) ........................... . For dinner I had
(5) ........................... and (6) ........................... ,
then (7) ........................... with (8) ........................... ,
followed by (9) ........................... .

**146** Do you have a healthy lifestyle? Doctors advise us to take regular exercise and to eat at least five portions of fruit or vegetables every day. Look at what Lizzie wrote. Write down what you ate yesterday.

**DIARY**        **Date:** ...........................

**147** There are mistakes in seven of these sentences. Correct the sentences where necessary.
Write 'OK' if the sentence is already correct.

1 You need a permission from your teacher to use this software.   _you need permission_
2 We're looking for a flat to rent.   _OK_
3 I'm late because the traffics are awful.   ........................
4 He was asked to leave the club because of a bad behaviour.   ........................
5 I phoned my brother to wish him good luck in the exam.   ........................
6 It's a pity Rebecca had her hairs cut so short.   ........................
7 I like the flat but the furnitures are very old-fashioned.   ........................
8 As an old friend, may I give you an advice?   ........................
9 We need to get up-to-date information about flight times.   ........................
10 Cycling home in the rain wasn't pleasant experience!   ........................

**148** Complete the conversation with the words from the box. Sometimes you need the plural
(–s). Use some of the words more than once.

| case   day   experience   luggage   paper   room   scenery   weather   view |

Mary and Liz are about to go on holiday together. Mary has come to collect Liz in her car.

MARY: Hello, Liz, are you ready?

LIZ: Yes, just about. All my (1) ....luggage.... is here. I hope I haven't got too many (2) ...cases.... .

MARY: Don't worry. There's plenty of (3) ........................................................ in the car.

LIZ: Oh, good. I've packed rather a lot of things. I haven't had much
(4) ........................................................ of travelling in the mountains, so I wasn't sure
what to bring.

MARY: As long as you've got some warm sweaters for the evenings, and a good raincoat, you should
be OK. The (5) ........................................................ in the mountains is wonderful, but
the (6) ........................................................ can change very suddenly.

LIZ: Well, we've got a lovely (7) ........................................................ to start with.

MARY: You're right there. And I'm sure you'll like our (8) ........................................................ at
the hotel, because they've promised me the ones I had last year when I was with my brother.
Did you pack the guidebook, by the way?

LIZ: Yes, and I packed some (9) ........................................................ so we can do some
drawing.

MARY: That's a good idea. It'd be nice to keep some sort of diary too.

LIZ: Yes. We might make an album afterwards, with words and pictures. And I'm sure I'm going to
have some great (10) ........................................................ to write about.

MARY: Well, the (11) ........................................................ are like nothing you've ever seen.
And there's always music or something in one of the villages every evening. We'll buy the
local (12) ........................................................ when we get there and find out what's
going on.

LIZ: Well, I'm ready.

MARY: OK, let's go!

# A/an, some and the

**149** Complete the description with **a/an**, **some** or **the**.

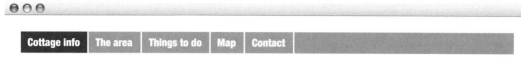

**Cottage info** | The area | Things to do | Map | Contact

## Grassington, Yorkshire Dales
HOLIDAY COTTAGE with amazing views
Sleeps two
Price range £300–£500 per week

The flat has (1) ....*a*.... large sitting-room with views over (2) ............................................. valley of
Wharfedale. In (3) ............................................. bedroom there are twin beds, (4) .............................................
large cupboard, and (5) ............................................. armchair. (6) ............................................. bathroom is
next to (7) ............................................. bedroom. There is (8) ............................................. shower over
(9) ............................................. bath. (10) ............................................. kitchen is modern. In
(11) ............................................. middle of (12) ............................................. room is (13) ............................................. round
table. Outside, there is (14) ............................................. small patio with (15) .............................................
garden chairs and (16) ............................................. fully-equipped barbecue. At
(17) ............................................. east end of (18) ............................................. road (about 0.5 km away) there
are (19) ............................................. shops which sell (20) ............................................. amazing range of fresh
local produce.

*plan of the flat showing patio, lawn, sitting room, kitchen, bedroom, bathroom, parking space, valley of Wharfedale, landlord's house 1 km, road, local shops 0.5 km, fields*

Now look at the plan of the flat and write two more sentences of your own about the flat.

21 ........................................................................................................................................................................

22 ........................................................................................................................................................................

**150** Write a description of your home or somewhere you have stayed on holiday. Use about 80 words.

........................................................................................................................................

........................................................................................................................................

........................................................................................................................................

........................................................................................................................................

........................................................................................................................................

........................................................................................................................................

**151** Put in **a/an** or **the**.

Tina wants to buy a car. She has come to see Ryan, who is trying to sell his.

TINA:   So, you don't say much in your advert. Is this (1) ......*an*...... old car?

RYAN:   Not very old. Come and have a look at it.

TINA:   Were you (2) ................................. first owner?

RYAN:   No, I got it two years ago.

TINA:   Have you driven it a lot?

RYAN:   Well, I drive to my office in (3) ................................. city centre five days (4) .................................
        week, but I don't use it much at weekends.

TINA:   I see. Now, the thing is, I'm (5) ................................. doctor. I've just started work at
        (6) ................................. hospital in Hills Road. I'm on call a lot of the time and I have to find
        (7) ................................. car which is really reliable. (8) ................................. car I used to have was
        always breaking down and giving me problems.

RYAN:   Oh, this one's very good. It may not be (9) ................................. fastest car around, but it always
        gets there eventually. And it's got (10) ................................. new set of tyres.

TINA:   Right. It's good to know that. Can I go for (11) ................................. test drive?

RYAN:   Um, actually, that's not possible right now.

TINA:   Why not?

RYAN:   Well, basically, I'm afraid it won't start. You see, (12) ................................. battery is flat.

# The

**152** Put in **the** where necessary. If **the** is not necessary, leave the space empty (–).

Portrait of a family: (1) ....._The_..... Campbells

There are seven people in this family. (2) ....._The_..... children
are Sandra, aged sixteen, Craig aged nineteen, and
(3) ....._–_..... young twins, Michelle and Ryan, who
are nearly seven. Their parents are Jack and Sylvia.
(4) ..........................other adult is Irina, Sylvia's mother.
They live in Brisbane, on (5) .......................... east coast
of Queensland, Australia.

On (6) .......................... weekday mornings everyone gets up early. Jack Walsh works for a company
which makes (7) .......................... paper. He leaves at seven o'clock, to avoid (8) ..........................
rush hour, and perhaps to avoid having breakfast with (9) .......................... twins, who are very noisy.
Sandra catches (10) .......................... school bus at seven-fifty. Craig is at (11) .......................... art
school, studying photography. He lives away from (12) .......................... home during term-time, so
he avoids (13) .......................... noise too.
Ryan and Michelle don't go to (14) .......................... school by (15) .......................... bus because their
school is just down (16) .......................... road from their house. After school, their grandmother looks
after them as their parents are at (17) .......................... work until six o'clock. Sylvia works at
(18) .......................... Modern Art Gallery which is beside (19) .......................... River Brisbane in
(20) .......................... city centre.

**153** Write a similar description of a family you know or a famous family.

....................................................................................................................................................
....................................................................................................................................................
....................................................................................................................................................
....................................................................................................................................................
....................................................................................................................................................
....................................................................................................................................................

**154** Read these news items carefully and cross out **the** where it is not necessary.

**PM TOUR** The Prime Minister leaves this morning for a tour of the Far East.
He will visit ~~the~~ Singapore and the Malaysia and then go to the Philippines, for a
conference about the global warming.

**ROYAL VISIT** The King Juan Carlos of the Spain arrives today for a short visit to
the United Kingdom. After lunch with the Queen at the Windsor Castle, he will open
an exhibition at the National Gallery in the Trafalgar Square and in the evening he
will have talks with the businessmen.

**RAIL CRASH** An accident has closed the main railway line between London and
Southampton. Several people were hurt when a train hit a bridge. The injured have
been taken to the Southampton Hospital. For the information phone the police on
01273 01023.

# Quantifiers and pronouns

**155** While you were on holiday, some thieves stole your wallet. You saw them, but they got away. Complete the description you gave to the police.

1 All _of them had fair hair_ .
2 None _of them was older than forty_ .
3 Both _(of) the men were wearing T-shirts_ .
4 One _of the men had a shoulder bag_ .
5 All _____ _ .
6 None _____ _ .
7 Both _____ _ .
8 Both _____ _ .
9 Both _____ _ .
10 Neither _____ _ .
11 Neither _____ _ .
12 One _____ _ .

**156** Use the words in the first box to make true statements about the people in the second box.

| (a) few (of) | all (of) | both (of) | lots (of) | most (of) |
| neither of | none of | one of | some (of) | |

| bands | classmates | cousins | doctors | friends | grandfathers |
| neighbours | parents | politicians | relatives | students | |

1 _Most of the students in my class like rock music._
2 _Both my grandfathers were farmers._
3 _One of the bands I like is Kings of Leon._
4 _Few of my friends wear high-heeled shoes._
5 _____
6 _____
7 _____
8 _____
9 _____

**157** Complete the sentences using words from the box.

> a few (of)    all (of)    any (of)    each (of)    few (of)
> half (of)    most (of)    much (of)    none (of)

1 It is widely believed that .....*all*..... human beings are descended from one common ancestor.

2 When Jill decided to sell her car, she phoned round her friends. But
.................................................................................... them wanted to buy it, so she put an ad in the paper.

3 Do .................................................................................... your colleagues give you birthday presents?

4 When my rich uncle died, he left .................................................................................... his fortune
to his cat and the other half to a distant cousin! We had never expected to receive
.................................................................................... it, but we were disappointed that he hadn't left
.................................................................................... it to us.

5 I think .................................................................................... children enjoy going to funfairs, although I
know .................................................................................... who are frightened of the big rides.

6 We'll have to work quickly because I haven't got .................................................................................... time.

7 Before mixing the cake, weigh .................................................................................... ingredient precisely.

8 I'll have to buy a new tie. .................................................................................... the ones I've got matches
this jacket.

9 .................................................................................... people enjoy housework, and I'm not one of them.

10 Brett lost his wallet, so he phoned .................................................................................... the shops he'd
visited. But he got the same answer from .................................................................................... place.
Unfortunately, .................................................................................... their staff had found it.

**158** There are mistakes in all these sentences. Correct the sentences.

1 He shouted at <u>all of students</u> although most of us had     ....*all of the students*....
done nothing wrong.

2 You can't borrow money from me because I have no.     ........................................

3 What happens if anybody get left behind?     ........................................

4 What a boring town! There are not good clubs, nothing!     ........................................

5 He was lonely because he had a few friends.     ........................................

6 I've wasted two hours because the whole information
you gave me was wrong.     ........................................

7 When I got on the plane, I was told I could have some
seat because there were so few passengers on that flight.     ........................................

8 Her problem is that she has much homework to do so
she has very little time for socialising.     ........................................

9 I feel so embarrassed that all know my problem.     ........................................

10 If I had lots of money I'd spend half it on a holiday and buy
a house with the rest.

**159** Choose the correct alternative.

**The place where I grew up**

Last week I visited the remote country village where I grew up, in a region now popular with tourists. I remembered the two old-fashioned shops and a number of old houses in the hills. I realised very quickly that although in (1) <u>many / few</u> ways it appears unchanged, in reality hardly (2) <u>nothing / anything</u> is the same.

(3) <u>All / Every</u> the traditional houses are there, of course, and (4) <u>both / most</u> the shops. But (5) <u>none of the / none of</u> houses are owned by residents. All of (6) <u>they / them</u> belong to city people, who arrive (7) <u>every weekend / all the weekends</u> in their noisy new cars.

(8) <u>Neither of / Neither</u> the shops sells local goods these days; they have expensive foreign food chosen by (9) <u>somebody / anyone</u> in an office (10) <u>anywhere / somewhere</u> who has (11) <u>little / a little</u> knowledge of the region.

There are (12) <u>few / a few</u> new houses too, and they have (13) <u>no / none of</u> local character. You can see the same style (14) <u>anywhere / somewhere</u> in Europe. In fact (15) <u>the whole / whole</u> atmosphere of the village has changed so much that it is (16) <u>any / no</u> more interesting than any suburban street.

# Relative clauses

**160** Can you answer the questions about the people in Box A? Use the information from Boxes B and C.

**A**

**1** Who was Mary Seacole?  **2** Who was Antonio Stradivari?  **3** Who was Ibn Battuta?

**4** Who was Marie Tussaud?  **5** Who is Valentina Tereshkova?

**6** Who was Katsushika Hokusai?  **7** Who was Joseph Niépce?

**B**

| Japanese man | Russian | Frenchman | Swiss woman | Italian | Moroccan | ~~Jamaican~~ |

**C**

> He travelled through Africa and Asia.
> He made wonderful violins.
> ~~She worked as a nurse and saved many lives.~~
> He produced the first permanent photograph.
> She opened a waxworks museum.
> She was the first female astronaut.
> He made the famous print *The Great Wave off Kanagawa*.

1   Mary Seacole was a Jamaican who worked as a nurse and saved many lives.

2   ......................................................................................................

3   ......................................................................................................

4   ......................................................................................................

5   ......................................................................................................

6   ......................................................................................................

7   ......................................................................................................

**161**  Complete the conversation with **who, that**, **whose** or **where**. If no word is necessary, leave the space empty (–).

Zoe and Pat are planning a party next Thursday.

ZOE:  Well, who shall we ask to this party?

PAT:  Oh, not too many. Just a few people (1) .....–..... we can be relaxed with.

ZOE:  Yes, I agree. So, who, for example?

PAT:  John and Jason, of course, and Carlo.

ZOE:  Carlo? Who's he?

PAT:  He's the Italian guy (2) .....who..... is staying with John.

ZOE:  Oh, yeah. Is he the one (3) ............................ wallet got stolen when they were in London?

PAT:  That's right. They caught the guy (4) ............................ took it, but he'd already spent all the money (5) ............................ Carlo had brought with him.

ZOE:  Poor Carlo. Perhaps the party will cheer him up.

PAT:  It might, if we ask the girl (6) ............................ he's been going out with.

ZOE:  Who's that?

PAT:  Celia's her name. She works in that cinema (7) ............................ they show all the new films.

ZOE:  But will she be free on Thursday evening?

PAT:  Yes, it's her evening off. That's the reason (8) ............................ I suggested Thursday.

ZOE:  OK. Who else? What about Nicky and Cherry?

PAT:  Are they the people (9) ............................ you went to France with?

ZOE:  Yes. If they bring their boyfriends, that'll be ten of us. But have you got a room (10) ............................ is big enough? My landlady says we can't use her sitting-room because we made too much mess the last time (11) ............................ she let us have a party.

PAT:  It's all right. Our house has got a basement (12) ............................ we store old furniture. If we clean it up, it'll be fine.

ZOE:  Great. Let's go and have a look at it.

**162**  Complete the sentences with your own ideas. Use a relative pronoun.

1  I like meeting people .....who have travelled widely..................................... .

2  I enjoy parties .....which go on till dawn........................................... .

3  I avoid going to clubs ................................................................. .

4  Most of my friends are people ..................................................... .

5  I never wear clothes ................................................................... .

6  My favourite films are those ....................................................... .

7  I feel sorry for students .............................................................. .

8  My best friend is someone .......................................................... .

9  I'm going to buy a phone ............................................................ .

10  I wish I had a job ....................................................................... .

**163**  Tick (✓) the sentence which matches the situation.

**1** I have three umbrellas. I bought one of them in Paris. That one needs repairing.
  *a* The umbrella which I bought in Paris needs repairing. ✓
  *b* The umbrella, which I bought in Paris, needs repairing.

**2** I have one colleague. He works extremely hard. He has few friends.
  *a* My colleague who works extremely hard is not very popular.
  *b* My colleague, who works extremely hard, is not very popular. ✓

**3** I have several aunts. One works in New York. She's getting married.
  *a* My aunt who works in New York is getting married.
  *b* My aunt, who works in New York, is getting married.

**4** Peter made some sandwiches. They have all been eaten. You made some too. Your sandwiches have not been eaten.
  *a* The sandwiches which Peter made have all been eaten.
  *b* The sandwiches, which Peter made, have all been eaten.

**5** There was only one park in this town. Someone has built over it. We used to play in the park when we were children.
  *a* The local park where we played as children has been built over.
  *b* The local park, where we played as children, has been built over.

**6** One of my French teachers helps me with my homework. The other one lives too far away.
  *a* The French teacher whose house is near mine helps me with my homework.
  *b* The French teacher, whose house is near mine, helps me with my homework.

**7** You met one of my cousins last summer, the one from America. He's coming to stay again.
  *a* My American cousin who you met last summer is coming to stay again.
  *b* My American cousin, who you met last summer, is coming to stay again.

**8** There were a lot of candidates in the presidential election. Three of them were women. The winner was one of them. She had campaigned for better housing conditions.
  *a* The woman who had campaigned for better housing conditions has been elected President.
  *b* The woman, who had campaigned for better housing conditions, has been elected President.

**9** I received lots of flowers when I was ill, but only my boyfriend sent me roses. I put the roses in my favourite vase.
  *a* The roses which my boyfriend sent look beautiful in my favourite vase.
  *b* The roses, which my boyfriend sent, look beautiful in my favourite vase.

**10** I took two cameras away with me. You lent me one of them. That's the one that got broken.
  *a* The camera which you lent me has been broken.
  *b* The camera, which you lent me, has been broken.

# Adjectives and adverbs

**164**  Choose the correct alternative.

---

**From:** Misha Kissin
**To:** Natasha Tchistyakova
**Subject:** Language school

---

Dear Natasha,

Well, here I am in England. Thank you for your (1) <u>kind / ~~kindly~~</u> letter. You ask me what it's like here. I must say, it's pretty (2) <u>good / well</u>!

The language school is very (3) <u>efficient / efficiently</u> organised. On the first morning we had to do a test, which I found rather (4) <u>hard / hardly</u>. However I got a (5) <u>surprising / surprisingly</u> good mark, so I'm in the top class. I didn't talk much at first, because I couldn't think of the words (6) <u>quick / quickly</u> enough, but (7) <u>late / lately</u> I've become much more (8) <u>fluent / fluently</u>.

I'm staying with a family who live (9) <u>near / nearly</u> the school. They are quite (10) <u>pleasant / pleasantly</u>, although I don't see much of them because I'm always so (11) <u>busy / busily</u> with my friends from school. I was surprised how (12) <u>easy / easily</u> I made new friends here. They come from (13) <u>different / differently</u> parts of the world and we have some (14) <u>absolute / absolutely</u> fascinating discussions.

I do hope you will be able to join me here next term. I'm sure we'd have (15) <u>good / well</u> fun together.

All the best,

Misha

P.S. Aren't you impressed at how (16) <u>accurate / accurately</u> my English is now?!

---

**165**  There are mistakes in seven of these sentences. Correct the sentences where necessary.
Write 'OK' if the sentence is already correct.

1  *'Please get a move on!' shouted Trevor impatient.*    <u>shouted Trevor impatiently</u>

2  *I believe she is a very lonely woman.*    <u>OK</u>

3  *I didn't like his plan, which seemed unnecessary complicated to me.*

4  *I'm sure you could win the match if you tried hardly.*

5  *I have an awful headache, so could you please be quiet?*

6  *Soraya's only been in France a year, but she speaks perfectly French.*

7  *The reason Bruce gets so tired is that he has an exceptional demanding job.*

8  *My mother was ill last year, but she's good enough to go on holiday now.*

9  *David ran as fast as he could, but he still arrived late.*

10  *Jean always says she's short of money, but I happen to know she actually has a very good-paid job.*

# Comparatives and superlatives

**166**  A class of students is studying environmental issues with their teacher. Look at the chart and complete their conversation.

**Smashing figures?**
**% glass recycled by selected countries 2009**

Belgium
Netherlands
Norway
Italy
Czech Republic
Spain
Portugal
Croatia
Poland

40   60   80   100

TEACHER: On this bar chart, who recycled (1) ...*the highest*... percentage of glass in 2009?

FLORA: The Belgians did.

TEACHER: And who recycled (2) ................................ percentage?

WAYNE: The Poles.

TEACHER: Right. What about the Spanish? How well did they do?

JILL: They did (3) ................................ the Poles and Portuguese, but (4) ................................ the Czechs.

TEACHER: Did the Croatians recycle a (5) ................................ percentage of glass ................................ the Portuguese?

KEVIN: No, not quite. About five per cent (6) ................................ .

TEACHER: What about the Norwegians?

BRONWEN: They recycled almost (7) ................................ percentage ................................ the Dutch.

TEACHER: Yes. That's over ten per cent (8) ................................ the Italians.

ALEX: But it's still seven per cent (9) ................................ the Belgians.

TEACHER: True. Now let's go on to talk about what we're going to do next.

**167**  The class in the previous exercise took part in a paper recycling project. Look at the chart below and write sentences comparing the students' achievements.

FLORA    KEVIN    JILL    BRONWEN    ALEX    WAYNE

**1** (Kevin / Flora / Jill)
    *Kevin didn't collect as much paper as Flora, but he collected more than Jill.*

**2** (Alex / Bronwen / Jill)   *Alex collected five kilos less than Bronwen or Jill.*

**3** (Flora)   *Flora collected the most paper.*

**4** (Jill / Alex / Wayne) ................................................................

**5** (Bronwen / Jill) ................................................................

**6** (Wayne) ................................................................

**7** (Alex / Bronwen / Wayne) ................................................................

**8** (Jill / Flora / Alex) ................................................................

**168**

Complete the conversations. Use the correct form of the word(s) given and any other words you need.

**A** JOE: Why have you bought a new car?

AMY: We needed one with a (1) _bigger_ (big) boot, to take our sports gear.

**B** MARY: Which is (2) _the highest_ (high / mountain) in Africa?

ANNE: I'm not sure. Kilimanjaro, perhaps?

MARY: Where's that? In Zambia?

ANNE: No, it's (3) _further north than_ (far / north) that. Kenya I think.

**C** ANDY: Are you still having problems with your broadband connection?

JESS: Yes. I don't know what's wrong. I've tried contacting the server, but it's still

(4) .................................................... (fast) last week.

**D** ROSA: Which part of London has (5) .................................................... (cheap) flats to

rent, do you think?

ANA: I don't know. It's (6) .................................................... (expensive) city in the

country so they won't be cheap anywhere.

ROSA: I suppose the suburbs (7) .................................................... (far) from the centre

would be the place to look.

ANA: I'm not sure it works like that in London.

**E** FRED: How was your driving test?

JOSH: Oh, not so bad really. It was (8) .................................................... (much / easy)

I'd expected, in fact. And I passed!

FRED: Congratulations! That's (9) .................................................... (good) news I've

heard for ages!

**F** GAIL: Shall we go wind-surfing? It's lovely and sunny.

MICK: I'm not sure. The wind is good but I think you'll find it's

(10) .................................................... (not / warm) it looks when you get outside.

**G** EDDY: Let's go clubbing after we've eaten.

SEAN: Can't we go (11) .................................................... (late)? I want to watch a film.

EDDY: No. The clubs shut (12) .................................................... (early / here) they do at

home.

**H** WILL: Come on! Can't you cycle (13) .................................................... (fast)?

PETE: Sorry, I'm going (14) .................................................... (fast) I can already.

WILL: Yeah, your bike's quite a bit (15) .................................................... (old / mine), I guess.

**I** CHRIS: I hear you were having problems with your business last year. Is it (16)

.................................................... (good) this year?

JODIE: No. I'm afraid it's (17) .................................................... (bad) if anything.

CHRIS: I suppose people just aren't spending (18) .................................................... (much

/ money) they used to.

# Word order

**169** Rewrite the sentences using the words in brackets.

**1** We left early.
(the meeting) ....We left the meeting early.......

**2** We went to the cinema and we had a meal.
(also) ................................................................................

**3** My sister plays volleyball in summer.
(in the park) ................................................................................

**4** She's worked since she left school.
(for that company) ................................................................................

**5** If you order the trainers online, they'll be delivered by post.
(now) (tomorrow) ................................................................................

**6** He sends an email from his office every lunchtime.
(his girlfriend) ................................................................................

**7** When the flowers were delivered, was there a note?
(with them) ................................................................................

**8** We were late for work because of the traffic jam.
(all) ................................................................................

**9** I'm going to Zurich soon.
(definitely) ................................................................................

**10** The meal was lovely. My friends had asked the restaurant to make a birthday cake.
(even) (for me) ................................................................................

**170** Write three sentences about each of the three people in the left-hand column of the chart.
Use the words in each row and add the adverbs at the top.

|  | occasionally | usually | hardly ever |
|---|---|---|---|
| **Angela** | arrives at work early | isn't in the office at lunchtime | has been off sick |
| **John** | is late in the morning | doesn't eat with his colleagues | answers emails promptly |
| **Craig** | has worked from home | drinks a lot of coffee | is in a bad temper |

**1** ....Angela occasionally arrives at work early........

**2** ....John is occasionally late in the morning........

**3** ................................................................................

**4** ................................................................................

**5** ................................................................................

**6** ................................................................................

**7** ................................................................................

**8** ................................................................................

**9** ................................................................................

**171** Rewrite each <u>underlined</u> sentence using the adverb in brackets.

Andy and Jane came home from shopping on Saturday to find their house had been burgled.
A police officer has come to investigate the crime.

OFFICER: You say you're not sure how the thieves got in. Before I look round, can I ask you a few questions about the house?

ANDY: Of course.

OFFICER: (1) <u>Do you lock the front door when you go out?</u> (always)
   *Do you always lock the front door when you go out?*

ANDY: (2) <u>Yes, and I locked it yesterday.</u> (definitely)
   *Yes, and I definitely locked it yesterday.*

OFFICER: OK. What about the windows?

ANDY: (3) <u>Well, the downstairs ones are locked.</u> (always)

JANE: (4) <u>We have a lock on the little one in the hall.</u> (even)

OFFICER: And upstairs?

JANE: (5) Well, I think <u>most of the windows were locked.</u> (probably)

ANDY: (6) <u>They were locked on Friday.</u> (all)

   JANE: Are you sure?

ANDY: (7) Yes, <u>I knew we would be out all day</u>, so I checked them all. (both)

OFFICER: And you didn't open any on Friday night?

ANDY: (8) No, <u>I didn't.</u> (certainly)

OFFICER: Well, I can't understand it. Let's look round. Perhaps I'll notice something you've missed.

**172** Answer the questions using the words in brackets.

**1** What does Tim have for breakfast? (has muesli with yogurt + usually)
   He *usually has muesli with yogurt* .

**2** Why did James leave the party so early? (was getting bored + probably)
   He *was probably getting bored* .

**3** Does Maggie go to a gym regularly? (doesn't belong to one + even)
   She ............................................................................................... .

**4** What does Saskia think of your new apartment? (has been there + never)
   She ............................................................................................... .

**5** Do you know where Maureen might be? (has a few days off at this time of year + often)
   She ............................................................................................... .

**6** How is Keith getting on with his assignment? (has finished it + almost)
   He ............................................................................................... .

# Prepositions of time

**173** Put in **at, for, during, by, until** or **in**.

The city of London was founded by the Romans (1) ....*in*.... the year 43 AD.
(2) ....*During*..... the next few years it quickly became the main trading centre in Britain.
(3) .................................................... two hundred years after the Romans
left, the city was almost forgotten. Its full importance did not return
(4) .................................................... the eleventh century.
(5) .................................................... the end of that century, the government of
England was based in Westminster and the Tower of London had been started.
(6) .................................................... the Middle Ages London continued to grow
and (7) .................................................... the time of Shakespeare, it had become a
prosperous capital city with many fine buildings. Unfortunately, most of these buildings
were made of wood and (8) .................................................... 1666 they were
almost all destroyed by a fire which lasted (9) ....................................................
several days. This was a great tragedy for the people living there
(10) .................................................... that time, but it is true that many of the areas
which are most attractive today were planned (11) ....................................................
the rebuilding which followed.

**174** Answer the questions, beginning each answer with a preposition.

1 When's your birthday?
2 What year did you start school?
3 When do you usually have your main meal of the day?
4 What time of the year is it best to go on holiday?
5 When do you meet your friends?
6 When did you last receive a present from anyone?
7 How long have you been studying English?

**175** Complete the article with the prepositions from the box. If no word is necessary, leave the space empty (–).

at    by    during    for    in    on    until    while

# THE WAY PEOPLE WORK

**Erwin is a nurse who works the night shift. How does he manage?**

'Well, I finish work (1) __at__ 6.30 am. Then I go home, have a shower and try to be in bed (2) __by__ half past eight. (3) _____ the same time as I'm getting ready for bed, Joanne, my wife, and our four-year-old daughter, Elaine, are getting up. Joanne drops Elaine at nursery school, which she started (4) _____ last year, on the way to her office.

I usually sleep (5) _____ about three o'clock (6) _____ the afternoon. I have to be at the school (7) _____ 3.30 to collect Elaine. We come home and she plays or watches a cartoon (8) _____ I prepare our meal.

When Joanne comes home from work, we eat. If we're lucky, we can relax (9) _____ an hour before putting Elaine to bed. Then we do any chores that didn't get done earlier. I always allow plenty of time to get to the hospital because if I'm not there (10) _____ time, another nurse will have to go on working (11) _____ I arrive. I'm often very tired (12) _____ the time I finish, but I don't really mind. There's a special atmosphere in the hospital (13) _____ night. Of course, I have a free day (14) _____ every week. And the hours suit us, (15) _____ the moment anyway. I may want to work (16) _____ the day when Elaine goes to a different school. Perhaps I'll be ready for a change (17) _____ then.'

# Prepositions of place

**176**  Choose the correct alternative.

**A**  JAY:  Oh, look. Here's a photo taken in my classroom at primary school. Can you recognise me
(1) <u>in</u> / <s>on</s> it?

ANNA:  No, I don't think so. Unless that's you right (2) <u>in</u> / at the back.

JAY:  No, that's not me. I'm the one standing (3) in / <u>at</u> the corner.

ANNA:  In trouble as usual!

**B**  PIA:  I don't understand this.

LILY:  What?

PIA:  Well, I want to check something with the college, but it says (4) in / <u>on</u> this letter that I
must give a reference number when I phone, and I can't find it.

LILY:  It's in that little booklet, (5) in / <u>on</u> the first page.

PIA:  Oops! So it is. Thanks.

**C**  MEL:  Did you see Yves (6) in / <u>at</u> the disco?

JAN:  No, of course not. He returned (7) <u>to</u> / in France last week.

MEL:  But I'm sure I saw him (8) in / <u>on</u> the bus yesterday. In fact, he waved to me when we
arrived (9) to / <u>at</u> the bus station.

JAN:  How strange. We'll have to investigate what he's up to!

**177**  Put in **in**, **at** or **on**.

Hi Hannu,

Many thanks for agreeing to stay in the flat and look after things
while I'm away. Here are some notes about what's where, as promised.

<u>Key</u>
Anneka, who lives (1) ....<u>in</u>.... the flat (2) ........................ the ground floor has the key.
If she's out, the landlord lives (3) ........................ the building (4) ........................
the end of the street. It's called Laurel Villa, and the landlord is Mr Amiri. They both
know you'll be there while I'm away.

<u>Electricity and gas</u>
The electricity and gas main switches are (5) ........................
the wall (6) ........................ the back of the large cupboard
(7) ........................ the study.

<u>Water</u>
You can turn the water off by the large tap
(8) ........................ the corner of the bathroom. I hope you won't need to!

<u>Phone numbers</u>
I've made a list of all the useful phone numbers I can think of, for takeaway pizzas,
taxi, etc. It's stuck (9) ........................ the kitchen door.

I hope you have a good time.

Shiv

**178** Choose the correct alternative.

---

**TROUBLE AT NORTON MINING**

The workforce of Norton Mining has gone (1) <u>on</u> / <del>in</del> strike following a serious accident at the mine in Midsummer Valley in Virginia. The cause (2) <u>for</u> / <u>of</u> the accident is unclear, but miners are blaming management attitudes (3) <u>on</u> / <u>to</u> safety regulations. Damage (4) <u>of</u> / <u>to</u> equipment was frequently ignored and miners' demands (5) <u>for</u> / <u>of</u> safer working practices were rejected by the owner, John Norton. His relationship, (6) <u>with</u> / <u>to</u> the workforce was said to be very poor. Although there had recently been a rise (7) <u>of</u> / <u>in</u> the number of minor accidents, he claimed there was no need (8) <u>for</u> / <u>of</u> a change in working practices. Norton is away (9) <u>on</u> / <u>in</u> a business trip. A member of the office staff said she had spoken briefly to him (10) <u>by</u> / <u>on</u> the phone. The news of the accident had come (11) <u>like</u> / <u>as</u> a great shock to everyone in the office, she added. She was unable to say when he would be back. It is understood that the police would like to speak to Mr Norton in connection (12) <u>with</u> / <u>to</u> a number of his financial dealings.

---

**179** Complete the answers. Use the words in brackets with one of the prepositions from the box and any other words you need.

> as   at   by   in   like   on

**1** What's this room? (store room)
We use it ….. *as a store room* …… .

**2** What would you like to do now? (shade)
Let's sit ……………………………………………………… .

**3** Why doesn't your friend eat bread? (special diet)
His doctor has put him …………………………………………… .

**4** Have you got enough money for your train ticket? (credit card)
It's OK. I'll pay ………………………………………………… .

**5** Was the exhibition interesting? (recent college graduates)
Yes. The works were all ……………………………………………… .

**6** Was your brother hurt when his car crashed? (20 km per hour)
No. Luckily he was only travelling ……………………………………… .

**7** Why are you writing so slowly? (capital letters)
Because I have to put my address …………………………………… .

**8** Why is your hand so swollen? (wasp)
I got stung ………………………………………………… .

**9** What colour is Danni's new bag? (the last one)
It's navy blue, ………………………………………………… .

**10** What are you doing in the summer holidays? (motorcycle messenger)
I've got a job ………………………………………… .

# Adjective / verb + preposition

**180** Complete the sentences using the prepositions from the box and your own ideas.

> about   at   for   in   of   on

1 I know someone who's brilliant _at playing the saxophone_ .
2 It's difficult to feel sorry ......................................................... .
3 Athletes always feel proud ......................................................... .
4 Most of my friends aren't interested ......................................................... .
5 Many people are nervous ......................................................... .
6 My mood depends ......................................................... .
7 I enjoy laughing ......................................................... .
8 Lots of children believe ......................................................... .

**181** Complete the email with the phrases from the box.

> ~~at remembering gossip~~   for giving up   in changing her opinion   of behaving   of Helen
> of her behaviour   of making   on doing   on their advice   with her   with herself

Hi Terri,
You asked me for news of Helen in your last email. Well, you know I'm completely
hopeless (1) _at remembering gossip_ but basically the situation is this – Helen's
parents haven't forgiven Helen (2) ......................................... law and enrolling at art college.
They thought she would rely (3) ......................................... , but she says she's capable
(4) ......................................... her own decisions. Her parents have always been very tolerant
(5) ......................................... but they're really annoyed (6) ......................................... because of
this sudden change of plan.
When she told me, I could see she was really pleased (7) ......................................... . But her
parents are quite upset, because they haven't succeeded (8) ......................................... .
Well, it's typical (9) ......................................... . She always insists (10) .........................................
what she wants. I wouldn't dream (11) ......................................... the way she does.
Anyway, that's how it is. How are you?

Love, Sue

**182** Match the beginning of each sentence with the most suitable preposition. Then use your
own ideas to complete the sentence.

| | | | | | |
|---|---|---|---|---|---|
| 1 The lorry collided | 1 | _b_ | a of | ......................................... | . |
| 2 The bus crashed | 2 | ............ | b with | _a car_ | . |
| 3 The square was full | 3 | ............ | c from | ......................................... | . |
| 4 The minibus belonged | 4 | ............ | d on | ......................................... | . |
| 5 They borrowed the car | 5 | ............ | e into | ......................................... | . |
| 6 They blamed the accident | 6 | ............ | f to | ......................................... | . |
| 7 The owner was upset | 7 | ............ | g for | ......................................... | . |
| 8 The driver apologised | 8 | ............ | h about | ......................................... | . |

# Phrasal verbs

**183**  Write a sentence for each picture. Use **going to** + a phrasal verb.

1  He _'s going to throw them away_ .

2  She's .

3  She's .

4  He's .

5  She's .

6  He's .

7  He's .

8  She's .

**184**  Complete each sentence with a preposition.

1 I'm looking forward ....*to*.... seeing my family again.
2 My uncle ran away ........................... home when he was a teenager.
3 Have you ever fallen out ........................... any of your neighbours?
4 How well does your brother get on ........................... his classmates?
5 My dentist has told me that I must cut down ........................... sweets.
6 We went up ........................... a woman and asked her for directions.
7 My brother pointed his boss out ........................... me as she came into the restaurant.
8 The new manager came up ........................... several interesting suggestions.
9 I'll get back ........................... you as soon as I've got any news.
10 My brother gets away ........................... all sorts of things I wouldn't be allowed to do.

**185**  Complete each sentence with the correct form of **get** + one of the words from the box. Use one of the words twice.

( away  back  by  in  on  out )

1 The taxi stopped and a small boy ....*got out*...., holding a bunch of flowers.
2 We haven't had a holiday yet this year. We've been too busy to ........................... .
3 What time do you think you'll ........................... here after the party?
4 The festival organisers employ security guards to prevent people ........................... without tickets.
5 It's natural for parents to wonder how their children ........................... when they're away at university.
6 Modern buses are designed to make it easy for passengers to ........................... .
7 I don't earn much, but I try to ........................... without borrowing.

**186**  Complete each sentence with the correct form of **take** + one of the words from the box. Use two of the words twice.

( away  down  in  off  up )

1 The woman ....*took off*.... her jacket and began work.
2 I had to pay £100 to have my old car ........................... .
3 Few of the criminals ........................... by the policeman's attempt to disguise himself as a beggar.
4 The students were told to ........................... the posters which they had hung from their windows.
5 My mother ........................... yoga last year to keep herself fit.
6 I don't keep a lot of movies on my laptop because they ........................... too much memory.
7 We were offered drinks soon after the plane ........................... .

**187** Complete each sentence with the correct form of **go** + one of the words from the box. Use two of the words twice.

> away    back    in    on    out

1 I know the house isn't empty because I saw a man ......*go in*...... about an hour ago.
2 I don't know what ................................ in that classroom, but they're making a lot of noise, whatever it is!
3 I'm sorry I interrupted you. What were you saying? Please ................................ .
4 He was born in Scotland, but it's unlikely he ................................ to live there because he's lived in London for so long.
5 I'm sorry, you can't see the manager because he ................................ on business for a few days.
6 The green light on the front of the dishwasher ................................ . Does that mean it's finished?
7 I ................................ for a walk but if you need anything you can text me.

**188** Complete each sentence with the correct form of **put** + one of the words from the box. Use one of the words three times.

> back    down    off    on    out

1 One fire officer was slightly injured while ......*putting out*...... the fire in the hotel.
2 We have to allow plenty of time after swimming for the children to dry themselves and ................................ their clothes.
3 After cleaning, the paintings must ................................ in exactly the same places on the wall.
4 Is it OK to ................................ some music, or will it disturb you?
5 We'll have to ................................ the barbecue till another day if the weather doesn't improve.
6 Please ................................ that rucksack. It's much too heavy for you to carry.
7 It's cold in here. Shall I ................................ the central heating?

**189** Complete each sentence with the correct form of **turn** + one of the words from the box. Use two of the words twice.

> down    off    on    out    up

1 I always ......*turn on*...... the television as soon as I get home.
2 We didn't expect good weather yesterday, but it ................................ quite warm.
3 I hadn't seen Fernando since we were students, then one day he ................................ and asked me to have lunch with him.
4 We weren't aware of it, but it ................................ that we had been staying at the same campsite as our friends.
5 Can you ................................ the volume? It's very quiet.
6 When the captain ................................ the engine, we could hear the birds in the trees by the river.
7 Go and ask your grandfather to ................................ his radio. It's far too loud.

**190** Complete the announcement with the verbs from the box in the correct form and the words in brackets.

| cross out | fill in | hand back | ~~hand out~~ |
| hold up | leave out | rub out | tear up |

'Ladies and gentlemen, we will arrive at our next destination in three hours. At this port some passengers will need visas. In a few minutes members of the crew (1) _will hand out landing cards_ (landing cards). Please read the card carefully to check whether you need to (2) _____ (it). If you do not need the card, please (3) _____ (not / it), but (4) _____ (it) immediately to the crew member. When completing the card, be careful not to (5) _____ (any information). If you make a mistake, (6) _____ (it) neatly. Please do not try to (7) _____ (it) with an eraser. Failure to complete the form correctly will result in our whole group (8) _____ at the immigration office, so please read through what you have written. Thank you.'

**191** Complete the newspaper article with the verbs from the box in the correct form and the words in brackets.

| break down | bring up | fall out with | find out | keep away |
| let down | put up with | run away from | show off | ~~split up~~ |

# STAR ADMITS HEARTBREAK

Friends of TV celebrity couple Rosie and Jeff have confirmed that they (1) _are splitting up_ . They say Rosie (2) _____ that Jeff is seeing another woman. 'The relationship (3) _____ ,' revealed a tearful Rosie. 'I'm not prepared to (4) _____ him any longer,' she added. 'He (5) _____ in nightclubs and he (6) _____

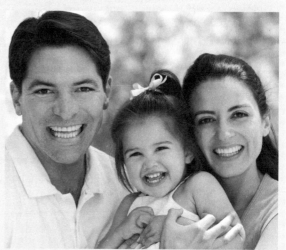

(me) in front of my friends.' Rosie plans to (7) _____ (their daughter Mimi) on her own, but she (8) _____ (not / her) from Jeff. 'Just because we (9) _____ each other, it doesn't mean he can (10) _____ his responsibilities to Mimi,' she said. Rosie hopes to find love again but, for now, she wants to spend time with her family.

**192** Complete the news item with the verbs from the box in the correct form and the words in brackets.

| bring up | close down | do up | hold up | pay back | rip off | ~~set up~~ |

# LAST CALL FOR HITTRONICS.COM

Talks are being held with suppliers of Hittronics.com, the high street company which (1) __was set up__ by Antonia Highbridge only three years ago with £20m of her family's money. Her billionaire parents say she must (2) ........................................... (them) this month or her business will have to (3) ........................................... .

Customers have claimed that Highbridge (4) ........................................... (them) with poor goods and inefficient service. Highbridge stated yesterday that her problems began because her business development plans (5) ........................................... by the family's attitude. 'Our stores look dated and I asked for extra capital so that we can (6) ........................................... (them). But every time I (7) ........................................... (the subject), the family said I had to wait.'

**193** Complete the newspaper article with the verbs from the box in the correct form.

| blow up | ~~break down~~ | drive away | drop off | give up | go off | go on | ride off |

# NOISES IN THE NIGHT

Residents of Victoria Street in Thornton were disturbed last night by an unusual accident. At eleven o'clock a car (1) __broke down__ near the end of the street and the driver left his vehicle there while he (2) ........................................... with his journey by taxi. An hour later, the car's alarm (3) ........................................... when it was hit by a stolen van. The engine of the van (4) ........................................... , so the thief tried to (5) ........................................... in the car. But he (6) ........................................... when the car wouldn't start and stole a bicycle instead. 'I (7) ........................................... to sleep at about midnight,' said Michael Patel who lives at 11 Victoria Street, 'then I was woken by a terrible ringing and a loud bang. When I looked out of my window, I saw a man (8) ........................................... on my bicycle!'

**194** Rewrite the sentences replacing the <u>underlined</u> verbs with the verbs from the box in the correct form.

| carry on | cut down | find out | leave out | ~~look back on~~ |
|---|---|---|---|---|
| plug in | put off | put up with | turn down | work out |

1 I'm sure we'll all <u>remember</u> this holiday with great pleasure.
   *I'm sure we'll all look back on this holiday with great pleasure.*

2 He <u>calculated</u> that it would cost $100,000 to do a degree in the States.

3 This lead should be <u>connected</u> to the back of your computer.

4 You have <u>omitted</u> several important facts in your report.

5 We can't <u>continue</u> if you won't co-operate.

6 He was offered a new job, but he <u>refused</u> it because he didn't want to move house.

7 We moved house because we couldn't <u>bear</u> the noise from the motorway any longer.

8 He had to leave when his boss <u>discovered</u> what he had been doing.

9 Potential customers were <u>discouraged</u> by the difficulty of parking near the restaurant.

10 The company has succeeded in <u>reducing</u> the packaging it uses by twenty-five per cent.

**195** Rewrite this email using the verbs from the box in the correct form.

| come up with | drop out of | get away with | ~~get out of~~ | let down | put up with |
|---|---|---|---|---|---|

Hi Mac, how are you? I'm fed up. I have to work hard but my cousin
Ruth is so spoilt. She always manages to <u>avoid</u> anything difficult.    *get out of*
She used to invent all kinds of excuses when she was younger.
Now she's left college without finishing her course. Her father
says he won't tolerate her behaviour any longer, but I bet Ruth
won't be punished for it, as usual.
If I disappointed my parents like she does, I'd be in real trouble!
See you soon, Ali

**196** Complete the sentences with suitable verbs in the correct form.

1 If you're offered the job, surely you won't ....*turn*.... it down?

2 Never ........................ off until tomorrow what you can do today.

3 The departure of the plane ........................ up by poor weather.

4 I ........................ out the mistake and wrote the correct word.

5 My cousins ........................ up by their grandmother as their parents worked abroad.

6 The festival blamed the mistake on the ticket agency, who ........................ them down.

7 I'm no good at ........................ up stories, but I'll read you one if you like.

8 A cat got into the museum and ........................ off the burglar alarm.

**197** Complete each answer with a suitable phrasal verb + a pronoun where necessary.

1 NINA: What shall I do about this form on the website?

   JOHN: Just ....*fill it in*.... online and click 'send'.

2 FRED: Is Sonia a fast runner?

   SUE: Oh, yes. Nobody else on the team can ........................ .

3 ALAN: Why didn't you buy a new computer game?

   DAVE: The shop has ........................ the latest ones.

4 MAY: Did you believe Nicola's story?

   EVAN: No, I knew she must have ........................ .

5 GREG: Do we need to make a sauce for dinner this evening?

   BILL: Yes, so you'd better ........................ .

6 CILLA: What are the girls doing in the garden with the tent?

   ALEC: They want to ........................ before they go away, to check
   that it's OK.

7 LEE: Were you disappointed that Graham didn't keep his promise?

   RUTH: Yes, we all felt he'd ........................ rather badly.

8 IAN: Did Francesca play with her cousins when they came to stay?

   JIM: Oh, yes. She ........................ very well.

**198** Complete the sentences with your own ideas. Use **on** or **off**.

1 I turned ...*off the television and went out*........................ .

2 The children set ........................ .

3 The lazy student put ........................ .

4 I tried ........................ .

5 Our plane took ........................ .

6 The girl switched ........................ .

7 The boys carried ........................ .

8 The teenagers showed ........................ .

**199** Complete the sentences with your own ideas. Use **up** or **down**.

1 The young businessman set *up his own company making computer games* .

2 My boyfriend turned ........................................................................................... .

3 The old lady put ........................................................................................... .

4 My grandfather took ........................................................................................... .

5 The workmen knocked ........................................................................................... .

6 The gangsters beat ........................................................................................... .

7 The young couple were saving ........................................................................................... .

8 The business closed ........................................................................................... .

**200** Complete the sentences with your own ideas. Use **in** or **out**.

1 We often eat *out on Saturday evenings* .

2 The prisoner climbed ........................................................................................... .

3 The new student joined ........................................................................................... .

4 Air travellers must check ........................................................................................... .

5 The picture has been cut ........................................................................................... .

6 The schoolboy let ........................................................................................... .

7 My secretary will sort ........................................................................................... .

8 The investigation was carried ........................................................................................... .

---

**Solution to Exercise 143**

9.05 Lucy left the study.

Trevor phoned Gerald.

9.15 Lucy saw Gerald on the phone.

Delia and Doctor Emerson heard Trevor shouting at Gerald, on the phone. When he was checking the accounts, he discovered that Gerald had been stealing from the business.

9.25 Doctor Emerson left, banging the front door.

9.30 Gerald entered the house and killed Trevor after a short argument.

9.40 Gerald left the house and met Lucy on her way home.